Presen

From

Date

"Follow my example, as I follow the example of Christ."
1 Corinthians 11:1 NIV

DEVOTED TO JESUS

From FIRST STEPS *to* FULLY SURRENDERED

STEPHEN KENDRICK
and ALEX KENDRICK
with Lawrence Kimbrough

979-8-3845-0072-8

Published by B&H Publishing Group
Brentwood, Tennessee

Dewey Decimal Classification: 248.4
CHRISTIAN LIFE / EVANGELISTIC WORK / CONVERT

1 2 3 4 5 6 7 • 28 27 26 25 24

CONTENTS

Part IV: SCRIPTURE

Part V: CHURCH

Part VI: PRAYER

Part VII: SURRENDER

Part X: DISCIPLESHIP

INTRODUCTION

Jesus Christ has not only changed millions of lives over thousands of years but our own personal lives and families as well, radically for the good. After growing up in multiple churches, serving for decades in ministry, and meeting incredible followers of Christ around the world, we can testify that God is powerfully at work in this generation and is never confined to any one church tradition or denomination. His grace is still amazing and overwhelming.

We've watched Him set drug addicts free, resurrect dead marriages, heal deep emotional wounds, deliver relatives from depression, and transform students during a revival. He can do anything and save anyone who is willing to humble themselves and trust Him with their lives. Watching God's Spirit turn the light on in someone's heart and see their faith in Christ awaken is one of the most amazing experiences on earth. Then to see them grow and learn to walk intimately with Jesus and lovingly pour their lives into others is incredible.

That's what this book is about: following Christ, loving Christ, and becoming a wholehearted disciple of Christ.

True devotion is holistic and involves everything we are. When we find something worthy of our whole heart and then fully devote ourselves to it, then it will fuel our focus, passion, and lifelong pursuits. Jesus alone is worthy of our whole heart.

We hope that's exactly what happens in your spiritual life as you journey through these pages. Don't feel like we are piling on more religious rules or increasing your already busy schedule. Let it help you slow down and sit at the feet of Jesus. Learn how to walk intimately with Him. Allow Him to love you and change you deeply and then greatly use you.

The Content. This book contains fifty-two chapters, presenting some of the most important teachings of Jesus and the Bible in short, practical segments aimed at deepening your spiritual life and powering your growth. It addresses dozens of vital topics: the gospel, assurance of salvation, identity in Christ, studying Scripture, praying effectively, overcoming adversity, pursuing community, walking in love, and much more. We hope it proves to be an encouraging and enriching experience for you. Our goal is not religious education, taught to you by people, but true spiritual transformation that comes by walking with God!

The Challenge. Keep an open heart before the Lord. Whether you read a chapter a day or one a week, we encourage you to PRAY before reading, asking God to speak to you personally, draw you closer, and make you more like Him.

We challenge you to READ the Bible every day along with this book. Consider starting in the book of Matthew and slowly reading through the Gospels, which focus on the eyewitness accounts and teachings of Jesus. He is the key to everything else in Scripture.

Finally, DISCUSS what you've read with someone else and share what you're learning in the process. The best way to grow is through relationships. Let God use this book as an opportunity for you to establish a new mentoring relationship grounded in life-changing conversations. We've written this book in a conversational style, like two friends talking by the fire. So there will be incomplete sentences. Intentional fragments. As if Paul is pouring into Timothy, someone he loves and is discipling.

The Hope. We are praying that Christian growth in this generation will go far beyond Sunday experiences and include life-on-life mentoring relationships during the week that fuel spiritual maturity and the spread of the gospel around the world. Though Jesus taught large crowds, He spent most of His time walking closely with a select few. The masses heard His words, but His disciples saw His life. They knew Him personally, felt His love, and watched Him behind the scenes.

Contrast that experience with today's digital generation, being physically disconnected from others and desperately needing meaningful relationships. They can find solid teaching online but can't share their private struggles or spiritual questions with a video screen. They deeply need someone who knows and loves Jesus to take the time to know and love them, to walk with them consistently while modeling a sincere devotion to Jesus.

Whether you are a seasoned believer or a new believer, this book is for you. As a discipling tool, every chapter is a discussion starter you can read beforehand or out loud during your times together. Personalize it. Mark it up. Make it your own. Test everything with Scripture. But don't give up and don't keep it to yourself. Ask God to show you who He wants you to share it with.

You can do nothing more important with your life than to surrender it fully to Jesus Christ, walk with Him in an abiding, daily relationship, and devote yourself to serving Him. Then you can walk alongside others so they can know and follow Christ too.

May God mightily bless you as you seek to know Him more and more each day. And may we all become authentic examples of Jesus to the nations and to future generations. We hope you take this journey seriously and that you enjoy it fully!

Let's begin.

Part I

FOUNDATIONS

Who Is Jesus Christ?

1

The Invitation of Jesus

What does He want with me?

Jesus stood up and cried out, "If anyone is thirsty, let him come to me and drink." John 7:37

Jesus Christ has given all of us an invitation we should sincerely and thoughtfully consider. He invites us into a living, loving relationship with God through faith in Him.

This relationship He offers is not common or casual. He has opened the door for us to know Him and walk with Him more intimately than we ever imagined. It's not a relationship that always promises comfort or ease. Some aspects of this faith journey may prove extremely difficult, harder than anything you've ever done. But the results of developing a genuine devotion to Him will bring about an amazing life of growth, maturity, fruitfulness, and joy.

This book is intended to help you learn more about Christ's invitation and ultimately to embrace the narrow path of being His disciple. As we begin this journey, we encourage you to take some time to sincerely pray and ask God to open your eyes, speak to your heart, and draw you to Himself through this experience, guiding you into everything He desires for you, into everything discipleship means. May the Lord be with you as you seek after Him.

Throughout His ministry, Jesus repeatedly invited people to come to Him with their greatest burdens. Those who suffered physically found healing. Those tormented by evil found deliverance. Those hungering for answers found direction. Regardless of their problem, Jesus proved to be *the* solution. As He met their immediate needs, they would often realize they could trust Him for their bigger long-term needs and their lives.

Jesus consistently offered a new kind of life. A life where grace abounds. Where ordinary people experience the presence of God daily and find lasting purpose and peace, regardless of their background or circumstances.

Once on the last day of a great feast, Jesus stood up and cried out, "If anyone is thirsty, let him come to me and drink" (John 7:37). He knew they were living with thirsty souls, always longing but never satisfied, and that He alone provided the lasting refreshment they needed. He was constantly inviting people to let go of their empty lives and freely receive what they could never earn: God's gift of life and love. Once when He spoke to a woman who'd come to a well to draw water, He told her, "Everyone who drinks of this water will thirst again; but whoever drinks of the water that I will give him shall never thirst; but the water that I will give him will become in him a well of water springing up to eternal life" (John 4:13–14 NASB). This woman's life was forever changed when she realized who Jesus was and that He was telling her the truth.

On another occasion, Jesus spoke to a generation worn down by legalism and regulations. They were exhausted from following performance-based religion. Empty rituals had become like a yoke of slavery to them (see Lev. 26:13; Matt. 23:4; Acts 15:10).

But consider the invitation Jesus gave. He said, "Come to me, all who labor and are heavy laden, and I will give you rest. Take my yoke upon you, and learn from me, for I am gentle and lowly in heart, and you will find rest for your souls. For my yoke is easy, and my burden is light" (Matt. 11:28–30 ESV).

He recognized they were weary and overloaded from trying to work their way through life and to God. Always trying but always failing. Jesus knew He would completely bear the weight of their sin through His death on the cross and that they didn't need to try earning their salvation any longer. They could find spiritual rest through simple faith in Him.

But beyond salvation, Jesus also invited them to start living differently, to submit to Him and become His follower and disciple. He knew those who trusted His leadership could have a much better path ahead. His imagery of taking up a "yoke" was familiar to His audience. When two animals, like oxen or horses, were yoked together as a pair to pull a plow or cart, they could handle significantly more and could endure much longer by working together.

This is where believing faith becomes a fulfilling life of service and discipleship. Where peace with God also becomes a fruitful walk with God. Where our souls can find rest in Christ, even in the midst of the work.

Jesus is inviting us to let Him be the strong one yoked with us. Walking alongside us. Helping us carry every load in life. We can accomplish anything He asks with less effort if we lean on His strength. With the Lord next to us, we will see ourselves doing things we never thought possible.

What a loving offer He makes. A permanent relationship with Him. And inside of this relationship, the daily power to follow Him, know Him, and become like Him. To live a life that gives God glory. That's discipleship.

Not just deliverance from sin but a life of devotion to Jesus.

We don't know what you've brought with you to this journey. But the Bible tells us God predetermines *where* and *when* each of us will live so that we might "seek" Him and "find" Him, because "he is not far from each one of us" (Acts 17:26–27). Let that sink in. Wherever you are living and whatever you are carrying right now is for the purpose of helping you *seek* God and *find* Him. To personally hear the call of Jesus to follow Him. To be in a relationship with Him.

Let today be the day when you lift your eyes, give your burdens to Jesus, and let Him lead. To find rest in Him and start learning from Him.

As we begin this journey, we invite you to do something you may never have done before: to call on the name of Jesus and ask Him to meet you where you are. To help you in every area of your life. To help you stop trying to do life, work, family, and ministry on your own. To ask Him to open your eyes to who He is and draw you closer to Himself. To meet you in some special way that is very personal to you.

He's inviting. It's time to get in, learn from Him, and follow Him.

Dear God, I call upon You in this season of my life because I need You. Take my burdens, strengthen my faith, and open my eyes to who You are. Help me to trust You and follow You with my life. Change my heart and teach me what it means to walk daily with Jesus and find rest in Him. Use my life for Your glory. I pray this in Jesus' name. Amen.

Going Deeper

Deuteronomy 4:7 • John 4:7–10 • John 14:23

2

THE LIFE OF JESUS

HOW DID HE REVEAL HE WAS THE SON OF GOD?

Jesus told him, "I am the way, the truth, and the life. No one comes to the Father except through me." John 14:6

As you begin, please pray and ask God to speak to you and show you who Jesus is.

There is no other spiritual leader or historic figure like Jesus Christ. He is considered the greatest person and example to walk the earth. Billions know His name. Millions follow Him. The entire life of Jesus sets Him apart as holy and special. Unlike anyone else. Worthy of our trust and devotion.

When Jesus said He was *the* way to God the Father, He was not being hateful or prideful. He was being truthful. The Bible says Jesus is the only Son of God, God's perfect solution to save us from our sins and provide eternal life (see Acts 4:12;

1 Tim. 2:5; 1 John 5:11–12). God doesn't owe us many ways to heaven, and humanity does not deserve or need more than one.

Almost all religions begin with one person rising up and claiming divine revelation. But if you lined up every spiritual leader throughout millennia who claimed to offer the way to God, no one else comes close to Jesus. What separates Jesus from everyone else?

Jesus alone fulfilled all the prophecies of the Messiah. Old Testament prophets stated centuries in advance that God's Savior, the Messiah, would be born in Bethlehem (Mic. 5:2) of a virgin mother (Isa. 7:14) and would live in Galilee (Isa. 9:1). He would be sold for thirty pieces of silver (Zech. 11:12–13) and His hands and feet would be pierced (Ps. 22:16). After He was buried in a rich man's tomb (Isa. 53:9), He would physically rise from the grave (Acts 2:22–32).

This is only a sample of more than three hundred prophecies Jesus perfectly fulfilled. Like His disciple Peter said, "We have the prophetic word confirmed, which you do well to heed as a light that shines in a dark place" (2 Pet. 1:19 NKJV). All the prophecies point to Jesus. Many were fulfilled at His birth or by His enemies, so He could not have manipulated them.

Jesus lived a sinless life. No one is righteous or can rightfully claim to be "without sin"—except for Jesus (Heb. 4:15). His virgin birth was required for His sinless life (Isa. 7:14; Luke 1:35). Jesus had the power to overcome every temptation (Luke 4:1–13) and He stands alone as "the Holy and Righteous One" (Acts 3:14). His sinlessness is what made Him the perfect sacrifice—not needing to die for His own sin but for everyone else. "[God] made the one who did not know sin to be sin for us, so that in him we might become the righteousness of God" (2 Cor. 5:21).

Jesus performed countless miracles. He didn't do just one or two miracles in the shadows, without witnesses, but daily for three years in multiple cities. He said, "If I am not doing my Father's works, don't believe me. But if I am doing them and you don't believe me, believe the works. This way you will know and understand that the Father is in me and I in the Father" (John 10:37–38). Humble and tenderhearted, Jesus demonstrated great compassion over human suffering and willingly healed anyone in need, whether rich or poor, prominent or unknown, including government officials and blind beggars (Matt 9:18–31).

Fulfilling Messianic prophecy, Jesus released the "captives," gave sight to the "blind," and liberated the "oppressed" (Luke 4:18). His miracles were "signs" revealing He was no ordinary man (John 3:2). Each type of miracle revealed a different realm of authority Jesus controlled. Turning water into wine, healing diseases, walking on water, and calming storms revealed His power over nature. Forgiving sin and casting out demons revealed His spiritual authority over evil. Raising the dead and coming back to life Himself proved He was Lord over death. He is "the resurrection and the life" (John 11:25).

Jesus died a sacrificial death to pay for sin. He was introduced at His birth as the "Savior" (Luke 2:11) and He repeatedly said it was "necessary" for Him to suffer as His mission (Luke 9:22). John the Baptist identified Jesus as "the Lamb of God, who takes away the sin of the world" (John 1:29).

All four Gospels describe Jesus' betrayal and crucifixion to pay for sin with His own blood, "as a ransom for many" (Mark 10:45). Centuries in advance, Isaiah 53 explained the meaning of His sufferings. And Psalm 22, though written a thousand years beforehand, reads as someone standing at the foot of the cross, watching Jesus die. His death is further verified outside of Scripture in the historical writings of Tacitus, Lucian, and Josephus, saying that Jesus the Christ was tried by Pontius Pilate and crucified on a Roman cross.

Jesus physically rose again from the dead. Christ's resurrection fulfilled prophecy and proved He was the Son of God. The testimonies in all four Gospels agree. Jesus was seen alive by more than five hundred people after He rose from the dead (1 Cor. 15:6). His fearful followers became bold preachers after His resurrection. They traveled the world to tell everyone, wrote the New Testament, and willingly suffered for testifying to His resurrection. "For if, while we were enemies, we were reconciled to God through the death of his Son, then how much more, having been reconciled, will we be saved by his life" (Rom. 5:10). One of the greatest demonstrations of this truth is when those who believe in Christ today come alive spiritually.

All of these are not just facts. They require a response—to believe in Him and follow Him. We need a God who loves sinners because we are sinners (Rom. 5:8). We need a God with the power to transform and cleanse because our hearts need to be transformed and our consciences cleansed (Heb. 9:13–14). We need a God who has power over death because we're all going to die one day (v. 27). Jesus alone provides everything we need.

Anyone who comes to Him in faith can be saved, regardless of their religious background or what they've done wrong. His love can reach all. His blood was shed for all, for the sins "of the whole world!" (1 John 2:2). "Everyone who believes in him will not perish but have eternal life" (John 3:16).

There is one God and one way to God. Jesus Christ is the way. His entire life sets Him apart as uniquely from God.

Absolutely everything. What sins and needs in our lives can we lay before His feet? Absolutely everything.

> *Heavenly Father, I pray You would magnify Christ in my mind and heart. Open my eyes more completely to who He is, and teach me to fully trust Him with each area of my life. Transform me with Your truth, love, and resurrection power. Heal my life and deliver me from all evil. Make me an example of Your love and a witness to the truth of Jesus. In His name. Amen.*

Going Deeper

John 21:24–25 • 1 Timothy 2:3–6 • Hebrews 1

3

THE WORDS OF JESUS

WHAT DID JESUS TEACH?

The crowds were astonished at his teaching, because he was teaching them like one who had authority, and not like their scribes.
Matthew 7:28–29

Jesus Christ's words are alive and continue to transform anyone who embraces and follows them. Unlike other leaders of religions, who claimed to discover mysteries on journeys of enlightenment, Jesus never went on a pilgrimage for truth. He didn't need one. At only twelve years old, He was already stunning the teachers in the temple, who were "astounded at his understanding and his answers" (Luke 2:47).

As an adult, Jesus alarmed the religious teachers of His day by explaining the nature of God, the law, the Scriptures, and life better than any of them. He not only answered their toughest questions but confronted their legalistic rules and ongoing hypocrisy as well.

So they angrily sent soldiers to arrest Him. But when the soldiers returned without Jesus, they answered, "No man ever spoke like this!" (John 7:45–46). His teaching confounded their minds and gripped their hearts, like it still does around the world today.

Think of it. Nations, governments, and millions of people have been deeply influenced by Jesus' words. If you read His first sermon (Matt. 5–7), you quickly see timeless insights and mind-blowing wisdom. He explains blessings, hidden sin, relationships, and unconditional love.

Jesus both comforted and shocked His audience with spiritual truth, humbling them and calling them to account. But He also shared the priceless secrets of God's kingdom while helping people overcome their deep-seated anger and anxiety.

Over time, large crowds in every region gathered to hear Him teach. He boldly spoke the truth in love, and His doctrine perfectly balanced justice with mercy. Judgment with salvation. Everything He said was golden and timeless. He shared both introductory milk with the young and then fed spiritual meat to others.

Jesus taught with unmatched authority. Not as theory but with certainty. He spoke as the mouthpiece of God and could masterfully teach on everything from prayer to matters of the heart, from marriage issues to friendship—not because He had studied them all but because He had created them all (John 1:1–5). He didn't just explain but commanded with the authority of God. He forced people to get honest and make the needed choices they were avoiding.

Jesus knew things only God could know and had firsthand knowledge of ancient past. "Before Abraham was, I am" (John 8:58). He already knew details of the future. "Take note: I have told you in advance" (Matt. 24:25). He could speak unapologetically about heaven and hell while clarifying what will happen at the final judgment. "When the Son of Man comes in his glory . . . all the nations will be gathered before him, and he will separate them one from another" (Matt. 25:31–32). He warned, "Not everyone who says to me, 'Lord, Lord,' will enter the kingdom of heaven, but only the one who does the will of my Father in heaven" (Matt. 7:21).

Jesus didn't discuss coming judgment as a tactic to motivate sinners but as a coming reality established by a holy God, confirmed in our consciences, and reinforced throughout Scripture. He said, "I tell you that on the day of judgment people will have to account for every careless word they speak" (Matt. 12:36). He knew the hidden sin in people's hearts and how to put His finger on it—not to condemn, but to help them come to Him and be forgiven.

Jesus revealed eternal truth. With parables, He explained heavenly reality using earthly illustrations, bringing a new spiritual revelation to people. But not everyone was worthy of His words. Whether talking to public crowds or privately to a few, His parables split audiences, giving spiritual understanding to the meek but confounding the proud and rebellious among them. The humble had "ears to hear" and received what He said. But anyone who couldn't understand Jesus had already closed their eyes, ears, and calloused hearts to God (Matt. 13:15).

Jesus would explain the kingdom of God using His stories. As He revealed God's nature and compassion, the truth would liberate those truly listening (John 8:32). Afterwards, people would realize that Jesus Himself is the "pearl of great price" that He spoke about (Matt. 13:46 NKJV). He is the Good Samaritan who had "compassion" and "came" to the wounded

(Luke 10:33–34). Jesus is the "treasure, buried in a field" (Matt. 13:44) and the "beloved son" of the vineyard owner (Luke 20:13). Some would finally realize that all the Scriptures were also pointing to Him (John 5:39).

Jesus' words changed lives. He didn't just talk about God but invited people into a relationship with God. He explained that obedience to His commands is like building your life "on the rock" (Matt. 7:24). If we ignore or disobey Him, we lose the knowledge we have and are held accountable for rejecting God's Word. But if we obey Him, we are transformed by Him. Then our faith grows—to know Him, trust Him, and love Him even more.

That's why He taught. To redeem us and show each of us the path to eternal life. To Him. To heal our spiritual blindness and reveal the truth He has been embodying since the beginning of time. He came to be "the way" and "the life" He was teaching about (John 14:6). To reconcile each of us back to God so we can spend eternity with Him. "This is eternal life," He said—to know "the only true God" and to know "the one you have sent—Jesus Christ" (John 17:3).

So as you approach the words of Christ, pray that God will open your eyes to eternal truth and to His loving invitation for you to better know Him. As you read the Gospels yourself, take them seriously and let them change you. Believe them. Trust them. Willingly lay aside anything that keeps you from receiving the truth Jesus shares or from carrying out His loving commands.

The apostle Peter concluded, "Lord, to whom will we go? You have the words of eternal life" (John 6:68). We too must listen to Jesus, not just to learn but to follow Him, be changed by Him, and to fully experience new life in Him!

Heavenly Father, You know me and what I need. Open my eyes to the truth of what Jesus said. Please help me love, learn, and yield to the words of Jesus in each area of my life, for You have given us life and hope through what He's told us. I pray this in His name. Amen.

Going Deeper

Mark 4:30–34 • John 5:37–40 • Colossians 2:2–3

4

THE CROSS OF JESUS

WHAT IS THE SIGNIFICANCE OF JESUS' DEATH?

"Even the Son of Man did not come to be served, but to serve, and to give his life as a ransom for many." Mark 10:45

The death of Jesus Christ on the cross and His resurrection from the grave are the central events of the Bible. The more you understand their meaning, the more you can grow in your love for Jesus and can rest in His amazing love for you. Today we will focus on the cross. Considered the greatest religious symbol of all time, the cross is on millions of gravestones, church buildings, and on jewelry around the world. But people rarely grasp its significance.

On a Roman cross in the first century, Jesus Christ of Nazareth willingly did what no one else in history could do. He shed righteous, sinless blood (Heb. 7:26–27). The only person who didn't deserve death—died. He suffered passionately in our stead, bearing the punishment of God's wrath against all human wickedness (Rom. 2:5–11; 5:9). This one act by one man forever changed eternity (Rom. 5:18–19). He fully afforded anyone who was guilty of breaking God's law—including you, including us—a way to be forgiven, spiritually saved, and reconciled back to God through faith in Him. This gift forever liberated us from the futile attempt to earn eternal life by good works or righteous deeds (Eph. 2:8–9).

The magnitude of what Jesus' death accomplished was very intentional and affects every generation. Before God created the world, He knew Jesus would one day need to be sacrificed for our sake. The Bible says it was "predestined" from "the foundation of the world" (Acts 4:28; Rev. 13:8). The name *Jesus* means "God is my salvation" because He wouldn't simply teach and heal but would "save his people from their sins" (Matt. 1:21). All four Gospels take you on a journey to the cross. Jesus was resolute that He came "to give his life as a ransom for many" (Mark 10:45). He knew exactly what He was doing. He explained, "I lay down my life so that I may take it up again. No one takes it from me, but I lay it down on my own" (John 10:17–18).

"Behold," He said to His disciples, "we are going up to Jerusalem," where the leaders of the Jews "will condemn Him to death and will hand Him over to the Gentiles. They will mock Him and spit on Him, and scourge Him, and kill Him" (Mark 10:33–34 NASB).

Why would God choose crucifixion as the means for Jesus to purchase our salvation?

The cross allowed Jesus to make the greatest of sacrifices. Great sin results in great consequences. Jesus wasn't merely taking a bullet in a battle but was choosing to bear the full weight of our punishment and God's pure and perfect wrath against all human wickedness (Rom. 2:5–11; 5:9).

Crucifixion was the worst punishment reserved for the worst criminals. It is known as the most brutal and bloody method of torture. The Roman Empire mastered it over centuries to destroy any opposition. It was designed to make dying as shameful and painful as possible. A condemned criminal of Rome would be stripped naked, beaten and whipped, and then nailed to a wooden cross through the nerve endings in their hands and feet. This produced shocking pain in their arms and legs.

Once the victim was lifted up and exposed to public humiliation, the suspension made breathing feel like drowning, forcing him to constantly pull up on his burning extremities to avoid suffocation. Criminals suffered in constant agony for hours, sometimes days. It was so torturous that Romans exempted their citizens from it. A new word was invented to describe this level of torment. Our word *excruciating* comes from the Latin, meaning "out of the cross." It is unthinkable that anyone would willingly choose to be crucified. Why was it so needed?

The cross satisfied the law's requirement for a blood offering. Since death was the wage, blood was the currency. Because the "life of the flesh is in the blood" (Lev. 17:11 NASB), God's law stated, "without the shedding of blood there is no forgiveness." (Heb. 9:22). But animal blood could never take away human sin (Heb. 10:4). A much more valuable currency was required. How priceless would an offering need to be to pay for the sins of the world? Only the blood of the perfect Son of God would be at that level.

It was prophesied the Messiah would be "wounded for our transgressions," openly shedding blood for our open sins. Also, "bruised for our iniquities," inwardly bleeding for our inner wickedness (Isa. 53:5 NKJV). Jesus took the full punishment we deserved to bring us peace with God. "For God was pleased to have all his fullness dwell in him [Jesus], and through him to reconcile everything to himself . . . making peace through his blood, shed on the cross" (Col. 1:19–20). Taking His final breaths, Jesus cried, "It is finished" (John 19:30). Our sins were paid in full. He had faithfully offered "one sacrifice for sins forever" (Heb. 10:12).

The cross revealed the depth of God's great love for us. What our Lord did for us is too overwhelming to fully comprehend. The Scriptures are clear about God's perfect motive. Because God the Father loved us, He sent His beloved Son "to be the atoning sacrifice for our sins" (1 John 4:10). Jesus was also motivated by love. He said, "Greater love has no one than this, that someone lay down his life for his friends." (John 15:13 ESV). He "loved us and gave himself for us, a sacrificial and fragrant offering to God" (Eph. 5:2).

There has never been, nor will there ever be, a greater demonstration of selfless love. It's the greatest sacrifice by the greatest one to meet our greatest need. The reality and glory of God's justice, wrath, grace, and love were simultaneously displayed through Jesus on one day (Rom. 5:6–11; 2 Cor. 5:21). The cross was not a day of defeat. Even before He was powerfully resurrected three days later, the day of His death was a day of complete justice, perfect love, and overwhelming victory!

Because of this, some of life's most vital questions get answered:

- Which spiritual leader should I follow? Look at the cross.

- Is God really good and merciful? Does He really love me? Look at the cross.
- What does God think about sin? Can He forgive me? Look at the cross.
- Why don't I need to work for my salvation? Look at the cross.
- How can I gain eternal life? Trust Christ and what He did on the cross.
- How do I remain encouraged to persevere? Fix your eyes on Jesus and the cross.
- How should I live? Deny yourself, take up your cross daily, follow Jesus.

Jesus paid it all. His cross says it all.

Father in heaven, I thank You today for the cross and the love You have given to me. Open my eyes and heart to its meaning for my life. I trust the cross as full payment for my salvation. Help me to live a life that is dead to sin and alive to God by Your power. In Jesus' name. Amen.

Going Deeper

Psalm 22 • John 10:17–18 • 1 Corinthians 2:1–2

5

The Gospel of Jesus

How does someone obtain salvation and eternal life?

"For God so loved the world that He gave His only begotten Son, that whoever believes in Him should not perish but have everlasting life." John 3:16 NKJV

Pray for God to speak to your heart as you read today!

After Jesus Christ died for our sins, He was buried, then He was raised from the dead on the third day, perfectly fulfilling scriptural prophecy (1 Cor. 15:1–28). These two epic events established the life-changing gospel message that continues to spread around the world.

The gospel is the "good news" of salvation and eternal life that comes through sincere faith in Jesus Christ. Considered the greatest news of all time, nothing changes more hearts, solves more problems, and brings more hope, joy, and peace than what God does through the gospel. Your personal spiritual condition with God is directly related to your understanding and faith in the gospel. Our mission as His followers includes faithfully sharing, explaining, and living according to the gospel message.

Now, let's take time to break down the gospel in more detail to process it more fully.

God created humanity for relationship with Him. People were made in the image of God to know, love, and honor Him. As humans, we have deep relational capacity above anything else on earth (Gen. 1:26–28). We are not evolved accidents. We've been masterfully designed with living souls. Our minds desire to comprehend God, our hearts long for His love, our consciences desire His peace, and our relationships move us to relate to Him. Every earthly father should be an introduction to know God as Father (Matt. 7:9–11). Every friendship should prepare us for friendship with Christ (John 15:13). Every marriage should be a picture of the faithful love between Jesus and His church (Eph. 5:25–33). But Scripture explains that we have willfully turned away from God, fallen short of our purpose, and failed to bring Him the glory He desires and deserves. "For all have sinned and fall short of the glory of God" (Rom. 3:23).

Our sin separated us from that relationship. Sin is a rejection of God's nature and control. God is truth, therefore lying is sin. God is love, therefore hatred is sin. God is faithful, therefore adultery is sin. But we can be blind to our sinfulness and our spiritual need (2 Cor. 4:4).

So God uses our consciences and His law, the Ten Commandments, to reveal it to us. Try to be honest and test yourself. How many lies have you told in your lifetime? How many times have you stolen? Dishonored your parents? Committed sexual sin? Jesus said lust is adultery in the heart. How many times have you lusted? Murdered? How about hated someone and were unforgiving? Have you idolized anything as more important to you than God? These are just a few examples, but only one sin makes us guilty. God's law exposes us and reveals we are very guilty and will never survive God's judgment on our own.

The Bible also says the "wages of sin is death" (Rom. 6:23). Wages are what we receive because of what we've done. We all have sinned against God and deserve death. Death is a form of separation. Just as physical death is the separation of our body from our spirit, likewise spiritual death is separation from our spirit and God. "But your iniquities [your sins] have made a separation between you and your God" (Isa. 59:2 ESV). Not only do our sins cause us painful consequences in this life, but they will also disqualify us from being with Him in heaven after His final judgment, if we die in that lost condition.

"For we will all stand before the judgment seat of God" (Rom. 14:10) where He will "bring to light what is hidden in darkness," disclosing the motives of our hearts (1 Cor. 4:5), judging the words of our mouths (Matt. 12:36), and testing the deeds we have done (Rom. 2:5–8).

God is holy and must reject all that is ungodly and sinful (Matt. 13:41–43). And because He knows all and is perfect in justice, He cannot allow sins against Him to go unpunished, or He would not be a good and just judge.

There is nothing humans can do on our own to reconcile the relationship. We are dead because of sin (Eph. 2:1). Dead people can't save themselves. Our religious practices and good deeds do not somehow erase all our sins and make us right with God. If they could, then we could negate God's justice and earn salvation without Jesus. This is not only impossible, but it denies the great necessity of what Christ did on the cross and it steals the glory God deserves. Without help, we are without hope. But there is very good news. God is not only holy and just but also loving and merciful. He has taken the initiative to provide all of us a perfect way to gain forgiveness and eternal life. He sent Jesus (Titus 3:4–6).

Jesus did for us what we could not do for ourselves. He lived a righteous life without sin. He perfectly fulfilled God's law. Then He took upon Himself the death we deserved and died in our place. Jesus satisfied the justice and wrath of God but also demonstrated the mercy and love of God (Rom. 5:8). Three days later, God raised Him to give us life and to prove He is the Son of God (Rom. 1:4). "For if, while we were enemies, we were reconciled to God through the death of his Son, then how much more, having been reconciled, will we be saved by his life" (Rom. 5:10).

Jesus offers eternal life (a reconciled relationship) to anyone who will repent of their sins by placing faith in Him. God's command to all people everywhere is to repent and turn from their sin to Jesus, trusting Him alone for salvation (Acts 17:30). Repentance is not a promise of future sinlessness, but it is humbly turning from sin to God for His forgiveness and deliverance from it. The Bible says, "If you confess with your mouth, 'Jesus is Lord,' and believe in your heart that God raised him from the dead, you will be saved" (Rom. 10:9). It may not seem real that salvation is a free gift, but the Scriptures explain that God gives it by grace to show how loving and kind He is toward us (Eph. 2:1–7).

Countless people have found peace with God through Jesus Christ, but we each must choose for ourselves. Where are you? Have you truly understood the gospel and placed your total faith in Jesus? If not, is there any reason why you would not do so today? If you understand your need and are ready to begin a relationship with Him, we encourage you to call on Him now. Just be honest about your mistakes and your need for His forgiveness. Resolve to trust Him and what He did for you on the cross. Then open your heart and invite Him to save you, fill your life, and take control.

Lord Jesus, I know I have sinned against You and deserve God's judgment. I believe You died to pay for my sins. I choose now to turn away from my sins and turn to You, asking for Your forgiveness. Jesus, I'm calling on You as Lord of all and am giving You control now. Save me, change me, and help me live for You. Thank You for dying for me and for giving me a home in heaven with You when I die. Amen.

If you just prayed sincerely and gave your life to Jesus Christ, then we congratulate you and encourage you to please share with others about your decision. We will discuss how to grow in Christ in future chapters!

Going Deeper

John 11:25 • Romans 1:16 • 1 Corinthians 15:1–5

Part II

Growth

How Do I Grow Spiritually in Christ?

6

Your First Steps in Following Jesus

I'm saved! Now what?

"Everyone who hears these words of mine and acts on them will be like a wise man who built his house on the rock."
Matthew 7:24

Are you ready to grow spiritually? Whether you've been a Christian for one week or two decades, your walk with Jesus should always continue blooming and bearing fruit. Some people grow more spiritually in a year than others do in a decade. The difference can be how quickly you dive into community, obey God's Word, and embrace your new identity as His beloved child. Let's talk about this new identity!

If Jesus is your Lord, then God is your heavenly Father. Salvation comes with so many spiritual blessings (Eph. 1:3).

When you heard the gospel and sincerely believed in Jesus, the Bible says God adopted you and sealed you with His Holy Spirit, who is the guarantee of your heavenly inheritance (Eph. 1:3–14). You have a new spiritual identity in Christ—you are God's beloved child. You can think, speak, live, and pray from within this beloved family position. You have freedom and access to God in prayer (Eph. 3:12). Other believers are your brothers and sisters.

God's forgiveness and love is freely given to His children (Eph. 1:6–7). You can now walk with Jesus daily, more readily turn from sin, and submit yourself in obedience to His loving commands. Your worship and service are no longer based upon your own efforts but on the Holy Spirit's power working through you. With the faith of a child, you should cling to God's *much stronger* hand, trust His *much greater* wisdom, and follow His *much superior* direction, rather than relying on yourself. This "faith of a child" mindset applies to everyone: new believers as well as seasoned followers of Christ.

An excellent model for rapid spiritual growth is found in the book of Acts. A large international crowd in Jerusalem was listening to the apostle Peter explain the gospel and how Jesus was the fulfillment of prophecy. Then Peter boldly challenged them to "repent and be baptized, each of you, in the name of Jesus Christ for the forgiveness of your sins, and you will receive the gift of the Holy Spirit" (Acts 2:38).

The way they responded should guide what we do today as well.

"Those who accepted his message were baptized, and that day about three thousand people were added to them. They devoted themselves to the apostles' teaching, to the fellowship, to the breaking of bread and to prayer. . . . Every day they devoted themselves to meeting together in the temple, and broke bread from house to house. They ate their food with joyful and sincere hearts, praising God and enjoying the favor of all the people" (Acts 2:41–42, 46–47).

They received the message, God's Spirit worked, and these believers grew so fast and strong spiritually that they launched the *first Christian church in history*, turned their cities upside down for Christ, and spread the good news of Jesus to the nations (Acts 1:8). How did they grow so quickly? Spirit-led devotion!

Faith in Jesus. First, they humbly responded in faith to the simple message of Jesus and entrusted their lives to Him for forgiveness of sins and eternal life. God responded!

Water baptism. Then they willingly followed Peter's instruction to be water baptized. We'll discuss baptism later, but their quick obedience to identify with Christ through baptism propelled their faith forward. God blesses obedience! Have you done this?

Devotion to Scripture. Third, they "devoted themselves to the apostles' teaching," which means they committed to actively hearing, reading, and obeying the Word of God. God was transforming them through the truths of His Word. We encourage you to devote yourself to His Word as well. If you don't have a good Bible, find a translation you can understand and start reading through the Gospels (Matthew, Mark, Luke, and John). Then read the rest of Scripture and keep going and growing!

Devotion to church. They also committed to meeting with other believers and worshiping God together. There's no perfect church, and neither was this first one, but God deeply blessed their unity. Every believer needs a healthy, Bible-believing church where they can consistently grow, worship, and serve with other Christians. Are you devoted to one? If not, find one that is unified, loving, prayerful, and preaches the gospel. And then go!

Devotion to fellowship and prayer. Last, they also met outside of church in one another's homes for "the breaking of bread" and prayer (Acts 2:42). This accelerated their fellowship as they opened up their houses and hearts to one another and began sharing meals, their lives, and prayer requests during the week (not just on Sundays). Formal church has incredible value, but supplementing it with smaller group fellowship in homes takes everything to the next level. It deepens the unity, trust, and enjoyment of all the relationships. Add prayer, and the whole experience increases in sweetness and effectiveness.

So whether you're a new believer or a seasoned follower, these same elements are still vital for your ongoing spiritual growth today. Pursue them. Pray for them. Don't put them off.

As God worked deeply in that first church, their spiritual fire was fanned by their mutual devotion to Scripture, church, fellowship, and prayer. This created a fertile soil, and God showed up regularly and blessed mightily! His sweet presence and power were evident to everyone.

In many ways, that's what this book is for—helping younger and older Christians experience God together, locking arms in fellowship and investing in one another. Growing stronger in the love of Christ. Transforming their communities while making new disciples. Watching God be glorified through it all!

So, looking back at the list, which elements are a part of your life? Which "devotions" are still needed in your schedule that you should pursue? What growth steps can you take *THIS*

WEEK to follow your perfect Father with some renewed, child-like faith?

Father, I'm eager to grow as Your beloved child. You've blessed me with so much. Give me the faith of a child so I will go wherever You lead. Give me a strong, loving community of believers to help me grow in You. May Your Holy Spirit fill me and guide me each step of the way as I step out in faith, fully devoted to following You. In Jesus' name. Amen.

Going Deeper

Ephesians 2:19–22 • 1 Thessalonians 2:11–12 • 1 Peter 2:2

7

THE BEAUTY OF BAPTISM

WHY SHOULD I GET BAPTIZED?

"Go, therefore, and make disciples of all nations, baptizing them in the name of the Father and of the Son and of the Holy Spirit."
Matthew 28:19

After someone repents, believes the gospel, and places their faith in Jesus, they should then follow Christ's command to be water baptized (Acts 2:38–41; 8:36–38; Mark 16:16). Baptism is a beautiful experience and is celebrated in almost every Christian tradition. It honors God, blesses others, and is a very important milestone in the journey of a believer.

For clarity, baptism is a ceremony where someone is dipped or washed in water to openly identify that they belong to Jesus. It is not the same as salvation, nor does it cause salvation. Many Scriptures state that our salvation is through faith in Christ alone without any additional works (Eph. 2:8–9; Titus 3:5; Eph. 1:13; Rom. 4:2–12; 10:9, 13).

"For with the heart a person believes, resulting in righteousness, and with the mouth he confesses, resulting in salvation" (Rom. 10:10 NASB). Baptism must be accompanied by a genuine faith in Christ or it becomes an empty ritual. Our faith is in Jesus and His blood, not in water (Heb. 9:14, 22; 1 John 1:7). However, a true faith transforms us and will lead us to willingly confess Christ in front of others and obey His commands.

Though He had no sin, Jesus began His ministry by being publicly baptized. This was clearly different from His dedication as a baby. Though He was circumcised as a child and dedicated at the temple, He was also water baptized by the prophet John to "fulfill all righteousness" (Matt. 3:15; Acts 1:21–22).

"After being baptized, Jesus came up immediately from the water; and behold, the heavens were opened, and he saw the Spirit of God descending as a dove and lighting on Him, and behold, a voice out of the heavens said, 'This is My beloved Son, in whom I am well-pleased'" (Matt. 3:16–17 NASB).

God clearly blessed Christ's baptism. It was a powerful, defining moment for Him and for everyone who witnessed it. At the end of His earthly ministry, Jesus told His disciples to "go . . . make disciples of all nations, baptizing them in the name of the Father and of the Son and of the Holy Spirit" (Matt. 28:19). They obeyed His command, and the church exploded in growth as God worked through them.

Sometimes it's difficult to know when or where a person believes in Jesus. But like a wedding ceremony, baptism provides a memorable experience at a specific place and time when we openly show our devotion to Jesus. There are many great reasons to be baptized, but here are a few:

To obey our Lord's command. Baptism is one of our first opportunities to show that Jesus is truly our Lord and that we are no longer the master of our lives. Many people in Scripture were baptized the same day they believed the gospel. Baptism vividly shows our submission to Christ.

To declare our faith. Through baptism, we clearly express that our faith is in Jesus Christ and in His death, burial, and resurrection. Just as all three members of the Trinity were present at Jesus' baptism (Matt. 3:16–17), believers are baptized "in the name of the Father and of the Son and the Holy Spirit" (Matt. 28:19). Our lives are also identified with the true, biblical God.

To illustrate our spiritual transformation. Just as Jesus went through a physical death, burial, and resurrection, every believer experiences all of this spiritually (1 Cor. 6:17). The visible imagery of baptism shows this invisible reality. "Are you unaware that all of us who were baptized into Christ Jesus were baptized into his death? Therefore we were buried with him by baptism into death, in order that, just as Christ was raised from the dead by the glory of the Father, so we too may walk in newness of life" (Rom. 6:3–4).

To share the gospel with the lost. When a nonbeliever sees a person baptized, they may also be drawn to Christ. Many times in Scripture, one person would believe and their friends or family would then follow Christ too. A Greek woman named Lydia (Acts 16:14–15), a Philippian jailer (Acts 16:30–33), a Jewish leader named Crispus (Acts 18:8) were all baptized along with their households. Who knows who might hear your testimony or see your baptism and be drawn to Christ as well?

To be introduced to the family of God. Being baptized is a "welcome to the family" celebration and an introduction to our new brothers and sisters in Christ. It's also an invitation for believers to pray for our new life in Christ, to help us grow, and to help restore us if we fall away from the Lord (Heb. 3:13).

To build up the church. Baptisms greatly encourage the body of Christ and powerfully remind them that their prayers are being answered, the gospel is being shared, God is changing lives, and their spiritual family is growing. It lets new believers participate in bringing His joy to His church.

To progress our growth and service. Baptism can be a game-changer to usher a believer's faith to the next level. After baptism, Jesus said we should learn to observe all of His commands (Matt. 28:20). Many people share that they significantly grew spiritually after their baptism. It is not empty symbolism. God always rewards our faith and blesses our obedience (Heb. 11:6; Luke 11:28).

If you have not been baptized since you placed your faith in Jesus, we encourage you to follow your Lord's command to do so. Don't be afraid. It's a wonderful experience. Jesus has done the hard work for our salvation, suffering the shame of the cross. It is our privilege to show Him and others that we truly love Him and trust Him fully with our lives.

Father, You are faithful and have a reason for everything You command. You have made a way for me to have life in You. Open my eyes to the meaning and beauty of baptism and help me to celebrate it through my life and in the lives of others. Thank You for caring so much about me, my church, and a lost world that You would give me this opportunity to declare my faith boldly and joyfully. In Jesus' name. Amen.

Going Deeper

Deuteronomy 6:24–25 • Acts 8:35–39 • Acts 10:44–48

8

ABIDING IN JESUS

WHAT IS THE SECRET TO LIVING THE CHRISTIAN LIFE?

"I am the vine; you are the branches. The one who remains in me and I in him produces much fruit, because you can do nothing without me." John 15:5

Even after believing that Jesus paid it all on the cross, most people falsely assume that living out the Christian life and obeying the Bible is still up to them. To their wisdom and willpower. Their self-control and self-discipline. This is a recipe for failure and has never been God's plan.

Religious thinking puts it all on you, as if the key is just to try harder and be more committed. But following Jesus is actually more about repenting of self-reliance, receiving from Him all we need, and then walking it out by His grace and strength.

Mature, fruitful disciples do not focus first on doing great things for Christ. They understand they can "do nothing" without Him. Instead, they focus on getting right with Jesus and walking closely with Him, relying on *Him* to do the great things through *them*. The apostle Paul wrote, "I no longer live, but Christ lives in me" (Gal. 2:20).

Gloves do not produce great works. It's the hands in the gloves that do great things.

Jesus explained the key to Christian living is the principle of the *vine* and the *branches*. He shared this epic principle with His disciples, and it forever altered their lives. Here it is . . .

Abiding in Christ is the secret to spiritual vitality and fruitfulness.

What is abiding? It is simply *remaining* in constant fellowship with God. Not only knowing Him as Lord and Savior but walking closely with Him throughout each day. Relationship and fellowship are too different things. Relationship is the permanent connection between the Father and His child. Fellowship is more about the ongoing closeness and intimacy between them. Abiding is not only relationship but fellowship.

Your fellowship with God should not just be on Sundays or during desperate need but moment by moment. All day, every day. Like a vine and its branches. For us to stay healthy, grow quickly, and bear fruit, we must learn how to abide in Christ.

Jesus said it this way: "Abide in Me, and I in you. As the branch cannot bear fruit of itself, unless it abides in the vine, neither can you, unless you abide in Me. I am the vine, you are the branches. He who abides in Me, and I in him, bears much fruit; for without Me you can do nothing" (John 15:4–5 NKJV).

Let His words take root in you. This is a major difference from traditional religious practice. People wear themselves out trying to impress God and accomplish things for God. They often end up failing and very disappointed. They are branches out of fellowship with the vine. But other people seem to live from victory to victory, bearing the words, attitudes, and spiritual fruit of the Spirit on a regular basis. How? They've learned how to abide—in Christ, the vine, the source of "life" (John 1:4). We have no power within ourselves. Apart from Him, we cannot produce even one thing of eternal value. Nothing that lasts. Nothing that God really wants.

We need Him. Or we have nothing.

We all know what happens when an appliance is unplugged from power. It becomes unproductive and useless. When a computer or phone loses internet connection, it's no good for pulling up websites or writing emails. Productivity plummets. We feel the urgency to reconnect quickly.

Likewise, our ongoing fellowship with Jesus is the connection we must maintain. Yes, we should work hard, but we must work while abiding, not *instead* of abiding. Everything we need and all the fruit we bear comes through this abiding relationship. And it produces not just a little fruit. Much fruit!

So abiding is the first priority of every day. Staying intimately close to Jesus. Constantly depending on His Spirit for everything. Enjoying Him. Finding satisfaction and strength in Him. Walking with Him. We invite Him into our every moment. We lean on Him. And as we do, fruit starts naturally showing up in unexpected and amazing ways.

It can be wise words, loving attitudes, blessed decisions, or helpful works, and they all bring glory to God. "My Father is glorified by this, that you bear much fruit, and so prove to be My disciples" (John 15:8 NASB).

How do we abide and stay close? Read John 15 and notice the following characteristics in it.

Staying clean (John 15:3). Staying right with the Lord, confessing any and all sin (1 John 1:5–9). Even one sin, if we're aware of it and refuse to repent of it, can hinder our intimacy with the Lord. We must stay clean and close.

Staying in God's Word. Digging into the Bible every day with an open mind and a willing, teachable heart. Jesus said, "If you abide in me, and my words abide in you, ask whatever you wish, and it will be done for you" (John 15:7 ESV). Stay in the Word daily.

Praying. Letting communication with God be ongoing. Starting and ending your day in prayer. Talking to God whenever you want or at any time of need. As we delight in Him and seek Him, He gives us our "heart's desires" (Ps. 37:4).

Walking in obedience (John 15:10). Staying in step with our Lord. Submitting to Him. Cooperating with His leadership. Obeying His Word. Following His lead.

Walking in love toward others. This is one of His main commands (John 15:9, 12, 17). It's not a rule to follow or a ritual to maintain. His love is simply what flows through us when we stay in loving fellowship with Jesus. His fruit is what we naturally produce and what people see. *His* character. *His* peace. *His* tenderness. *His* truth and wisdom. *His* loving care and concern. What matters is Christ living in and through us.

So stop beating yourself up for feeling fruitless on your own, for failing to obey the Bible, act like Jesus, or do significant things for God. Start *abiding*. Stop trying to earn God's love. Receive it and rest in it. That's how you start enjoying God's presence. That's how you begin living with spiritual authenticity. That's how you gain victory over hidden sins and stop being dominated and enslaved to them. The overwhelming joy you thought was reserved only for super-Christians is the blessed privilege of every believer in an every-moment, ever-intimate closeness with Him. By abiding in the Vine.

I praise You, heavenly Father, for seeking me and receiving me as a branch in the vine. Forgive me for trying to do things my way, by my strength, and not trusting Your heart for me and the supply of Your Spirit. I need You. Only through You can I do what You desire of me. I yield to You right now, abiding in Your love. Live through me, in Jesus' name. Amen.

Going Deeper

John 15:1–8 • 1 Corinthians 1:4–9 • 1 John 1:3

9

The Most Important Habit

What are the steps to a good devotional life?

Very early in the morning, while it was still very dark, [Jesus] got up, went out, and made his way to a deserted place; and there he was praying. Mark 1:35

As you pursue an abiding relationship with Jesus, one of the greatest things you can do is develop a vibrant time of devotion each day with the Lord. This is a private moment of being alone with God to enjoy Him and align your mind and heart with Him.

The purpose of devotions is not to check a religious box or to impress others. It's about meeting with God and intentionally seeking deeper fellowship with Jesus. It's also a practical way to incorporate some of the elements of *abiding* into your daily routine.

Jesus set the example of this. He "often withdrew to deserted places" to pray and be alone with His Father (Luke 5:16). He would get up "early in the morning" (Mark 1:35) or stay up late at night (Luke 6:12) for fellowship time alone with God. If Jesus consistently pursued and guarded this during His demanding schedule, then we should do it as well.

Devotions are great opportunities to receive encouragement from God and be transparent before Him. Many believers refer to it as their *daily quiet time*. Intimacy requires time. When people deeply love each other, they intentionally seek time together. Beloved children enjoy crawling into the arms of their father. Best friends pursue regular companionship. Lovers seek one-on-one time alone. And we are all of those things in our relationship with God. As believers in Jesus, we are God's beloved children (1 John 3:1), friends with Jesus (John 15:14–15), and we are called the "bride" of Christ (Rev. 21:2). We have every reason to pursue time with our loving Lord each day. And we desperately need it! So think of devotions as a daily opportunity for you and God to delight in one another and communicate honestly together.

Setting aside time to be with God is not commanded specifically in Scripture, nor is it meant to be a legalistic rule. You shouldn't feel guilty or condemned if you don't do it each day. It's really about abiding. As you grow in the Lord and begin to enjoy daily devotions, you will discover it to be a rich and refreshing time with Him. It has countless benefits and can surprisingly bless your thinking, attitudes, and actions in ways you would not expect.

There's no set formula or recipe either. But we want to share a few common devotional practices that people enjoy, hoping you'll find them helpful too. Consider the following as a simple starter guide you can use to launch this habit in your own routine. Feel free to adapt it to your own walk with the Lord.

How to have a devotion or quiet time:

Get alone with your Bible, a pen, and a notepad. Whether you go for a walk, sit in your car, or choose a quiet desk somewhere, just try to find a secluded place where you can focus and enjoy this time. For some, it's getting a cup of coffee and sitting next to a bright window in the house. As the morning sunlight rushes in, that's where they spend the first minutes of their day with the Lord. Find a pleasant place that works for you.

Prepare your heart. It's good to take a deep breath, be still, and remember that God is good and still in control (Pss. 46:10; 103:19). Some people start their devotions by listening to a worship song. Some people get on their knees and pray. Some lift their hands and praise God for who He is. Another good way is just to open your hands, close your eyes, and thank the Lord for His love and faithfulness. As you delight in the Lord, go ahead and submit yourself to Him, asking Him to speak to you through His Word and bless this time with Him (Ps. 119:18–38).

Read the Word of God. The Bible is holy and alive (Heb. 4:12). It's a river of timeless truths that nourish and change us. God's Spirit teaches, reveals, and comforts us through it. He also lovingly disciplines us through it, while "his hands also heal" and draw us closer (Job 5:18).

How much should you read? Many people read one chapter a day. Others read for hours. Consider starting with five minutes and then continue as long as you desire. You can read slowly through the entire Bible over time this way. Read at a pace that gives you time to absorb it, not just get through it. But don't just read. *Search!* Stay curious and ask questions. "Lord, what do You want to say to me?" "What is this passage really about? Why is it important?" "What does it teach about Your character? Your ways?" "What do You want me to understand or do from this?"

Write down key things you discover. When God speaks, we should cherish it and not ignore it. It can be extremely helpful to write down any important truths or thoughts on paper to capture and then recall later. It's also amazing to track how the Lord works in you and recognize His answers to prayer that you previously wrote down and expressed to Him.

Pour out your heart to the Lord. Pray about anything and everything that's on your heart. Ask God to help you remember and apply what you are learning. Then spend time sharing your needs, desires, and burdens with the Lord. Be respectful but get to the point. Confess any sin. Share any burden. Pray for the needs of others. Ask Him for grace and strength. Ask Him to fill you, lead you, and use you. Lean on the Lord's Prayer as a guide if you desire (Matt. 6:9–13).

Go do what He said. Be open to any changes in your thinking, habits, or schedule that you can incorporate from His Word into your life. It won't happen all at once, but consistent time in the Word renews us from within and transforms our thinking and our lives over time (John 8:31–32).

Share with others what God is teaching you. Expect your devotional time to overflow into life and conversations. It will improve your attitudes, bless your workday, and make you more aware of divine appointments the Lord places in your path. God is so amazing!

Time alone with Jesus is truly transformative. We encourage you to start doing this yourself, or to begin again. To daily delight in your Father, Friend, and Savior! Like a tree planted by a river, we can be constantly nourished by our time together (Ps. 1:1–3). May you daily abide and abound in Him!

Father, draw me close to You. Renew and refresh me daily with Your living Word, Your Holy Spirit, and with sincere time in prayer. Change my habits and priorities so that I make time for You. Help me to know You, walk with You, and abide in You every day. In Jesus' name. Amen.

Going Deeper

Psalm 119:9–11 • Luke 10:38–42 • Ephesians 5:15–17

10

Evidence of Your New Life in Jesus

How do I know if I'm really saved?

"Truly I tell you, unless someone is born again, he cannot see the kingdom of God." John 3:3

Do you ever question or doubt your salvation? The Bible is clear that God wants us to know where we stand with Him. He desires for those who still need salvation to recognize it and turn to Him in faith (1 Tim. 2:3–4). He also wants those who have truly been saved to rest assured that they are His beloved children and have eternal life (1 John 5:13).

Jesus repeatedly warned that people can be deceived about their spiritual condition. Eternity is too long to be wrong about this. So we are challenged to "test" our faith to see if Christ is truly living in us (2 Cor. 13:5–6). The book of 1 John beautifully describes specific things that will show up in the life of a true believer and reveal that God's Spirit has genuinely changed them. You can use these signs of salvation to test your own life and see if Christ is truly living in you.

SIGN #1: Open confession of Jesus as the SON of GOD. "Everyone who believes that Jesus is the Christ has been born of God." (1 John 5:1). "Everyone who will acknowledge me before others," Jesus said, "I will also acknowledge him before my Father in heaven" (Matt. 10:32). People say various things about Jesus, but an authentic believer will shout from the mountaintop that He is the Son of God. God in the flesh. Their Savior and Lord. Who is Jesus to you? Is He just a good prophet, teacher, or example? Or do you claim Him as Your God? Your answer helps reveal where you stand with Jesus spiritually.

SIGN #2: A lifestyle of OBEDIENCE toward God. "This is how we know that we know him: if we keep his commands" (1 John 2:3). Since salvation is a gift, obedience is not the *root* of it, but it is a *fruit* of it. We don't always obey God, but a person who's been changed by the gospel will have a growing desire to do what Christ commands. The Holy Spirit gives us this new inner bent. To obey and do the will of our Father in heaven. To live out God's Word and follow Christ's example (1 John 2:3–6). Growing believers won't obey perfectly but will obey *increasingly*. And it bothers us when we don't submit to Christ. Following Him is a sign of having God's name written on our hearts. What about you? Do you obey Christ? Is your heart increasing in a desire to see more areas of your life lining up with His Word? Does the thought that He is your Lord guide your decisions? If so, your obedience is a sign you are already God's child.

SIGN #3: Ongoing REPENTANCE of sin. "No one born of God makes a practice of sinning, for God's seed abides in him" (1 John 3:9 ESV). Everyone has sinned and will feel the pull towards sin; but "this is how God's children . . . become obvious. Whoever does not do what is right is not of God" (1 John 3:10). People do not tend to repent on their own. But the Holy Spirit helps God's children confront sin as a regular practice. How? He warns us to avoid it up front. Then He lovingly convicts us when we do sin. It grieves us. Then He urges us to take responsibility, confess it to God, and walk away from it. The closer we walk with Jesus each day, the more our desire for sin decreases and our ability to resist it increases. Over time, we will notice we are sinning less while enjoying victory more. Ask yourself, *How do I respond when I sin against God?* With a calloused heart or a convicted heart? The true Christian's answer is: "I confess it. I repent of it. I want it out of my life." How we respond to sin is another litmus test of our true spiritual state.

SIGN #4: Genuine LOVE toward other believers. "We know that we have passed from death to life because we love our brothers and sisters. The one who does not love remains in death" (1 John 3:14). God is love! When His Spirit enters us, He gives us a growing love for others—especially believers. Jesus said, "By this everyone will know that you are my disciples, if you love one another" (John 13:35). New life in Him blooms real love in us. Our increasing ability to forgive, to desire God's best for others, to be patient and kind, to show compassion and support in a time of need, is evidence that "God's love has been poured out in our hearts" (Rom. 5:5). How do you feel toward and treat other believers in Christ? Is His love alive in you?

SIGN #5: The presence of God's HOLY SPIRIT. "The way we know that he remains in us is from the Spirit he has given us" (1 John 3:24). We'll talk more about the Holy Spirit in future chapters but know this: if you've truly repented and believed in Christ, you've been "sealed with the promised Holy Spirit." He is the guarantee or "down payment" of your inheritance in Christ (Eph. 1:13–14). If He is truly inside you, He will begin to encourage, convict, satisfy, and strengthen you from within. He will clarify God's Word and produce spiritual fruit in your life. It's amazing. His ongoing presence is a shining sign of true salvation.

SIGN #6: The DISCIPLINE of your Father. Among the blessings of receiving the Son of God is being adopted by His heavenly Father. "See what great love the Father has given us that we should be called God's children" (1 John 3:1). But what do good fathers do for their children and not for strangers? One is to lovingly discipline (Heb. 12:7). As a Christian, you can expect your heavenly Father not to let you wander off without His notice. He will lovingly correct you when you sin against Him—not to harm you (though it may feel painful), but to train you, draw you back, and grow in you "the peaceful fruit of righteousness" (Heb. 12:11). Feeling His corrective discipline is a birthmark of being His beloved child.

SIGN #7: Trust in JESUS ALONE for salvation. "The one who has the Son has life. The one who does not have the Son of God does not have life" (1 John 5:12). False believers trust in themselves or their religion. A true believer trusts in Christ alone and what He did on the cross. Is your faith in Jesus or is it in your church? Good feelings, good behavior, and good intentions are not "bad" things, but they are completely insufficient for salvation. Good deeds don't magically erase past sins. The apostle Paul proved this. He had an amazing spiritual résumé (Phil. 3:1–5) but willingly laid all his own "righteousness" aside when he discovered that only Christ could give him "the righteousness which comes from God" (Phil. 3:7–9 NASB). So what are you trusting? Yourself or Christ alone? Your faith in Him is a signpost of His work in you.

These seven signs reveal a genuine saving relationship with Jesus. If they are evident in your life, then rejoice and rest in it. If they do not, then do not put off the loving command of Scripture to repent and believe in Jesus Christ and call upon His name for genuine salvation (Rom. 10:13).

Heavenly Father, thank You for showing me how I can know I'm Yours, even with the uncertainty I may feel sometimes. Show me my true condition before You. Solidify and anchor my identity in Christ. Grow these things in me as I grow closer to Your Son, my Savior, in Jesus' name. Amen.

Going Deeper

2 Corinthians 5:17 • 1 John 3:1–24 • 1 John 5:11–13

Part III

Identity

Who Am I in Christ?

11

Your Identity in Christ

Who am I in Christ?

To all who did receive him, he gave them the right to be children of God, to those who believe in his name. John 1:12

Your identity, or who you are, completely changes when you place your faith in Jesus.

For the better! It's truly incredible. You are no longer defined by titles you possess, labels of this world, jobs you perform, emotions you feel, opinions of others, or wrongs you have done.

You are now defined by God. The One who made you, knows you best, and loves you most.

The Creator always defines His creation. You are who He says you are. Period.

This is foundational to our walk with God. Our actions and words flow out of who we are. Apples always fall from apple trees. Being comes before doing. As God changes our identity and hearts on the inside, it will also affect what we say and do on the outside.

So, who are you in Christ? What is your identity? Well, let's start by saying it is awesome (1 Pet. 2:9). But among many good things, let's focus on four:

You are beloved. Love is not just what you are given but who you are. He loved us *before* we were saved; He loves us *now*; and He will love us *forever*. And having died to save us, He will not allow anything "to separate us from the love of God that is in Christ Jesus our Lord" (Rom. 8:38–39). Nothing can. Nothing will. Through faith in Him as your Savior, you have gone from being dead to being alive. From separated strangers to being His "Beloved" (Rom. 9:25). You are now known through the lens of God's great love for you (1 John 4:10).

Many people have a hard time believing they can be loved to any great extent, knowing the depth of their own brokenness and faults. Anyone can struggle to receive God's love or trust it fully. Our experiences of being rejected or deeply hurt by others can blind us to God's love. That's why Paul, praying for believers, asked God to spiritually strengthen their hearts so that they might "comprehend . . . the length and width, height and depth of God's love" (Eph. 3:18). God was already loving them deeply as His children, but they didn't fully realize or receive it. That's how God loves all of us. More than any parent on earth loves any child. He is the perfect Father, giving you perfect love, not because you have earned His love, but because He is love. The cross of Jesus is proof of it (Rom. 5:8). So let us "come to know and to believe the love that God has for us" (1 John 4:16). Believe it! Ask God to help you receive it and walk in it!

You are God's child. If Jesus is your Lord, then God is your Father. You belong to Him. You are not just a loved being on the other side of God's universe. You are now His child, brought near through Jesus as a welcomed member of His family. The Bible says you've been "adopted" (Eph. 1:5). Born-again Christians are "born, not of natural descent, or of the will of the flesh, or of the will of man, but of God" (John 1:13).

As an adoptive Father, He didn't merely receive you as His child, He intentionally set His heart upon you "according to the good pleasure of his will" (Eph. 1:5). No believer is an accident or an afterthought. He knew you long before you were born. He chose you in Christ "before the foundation of the world" (Eph. 1:4) and holds you still in His hand (John 10:29).

You are a new creation. Jesus didn't die to give people a facelift or fresh coat of paint. He radically makes us new. "If anyone is in Christ, he is a new creation; the old has passed away, and see, the new has come!" (2 Cor. 5:17). This is a deep truth: through Christ, God spiritually crucified our old self, buried us with Christ, and then raised us up new and alive in Him (Rom. 6:3–11). Beforehand, you were "dead in your trespasses and sins" (Eph. 2:1). You lived in the land of the dying. Spiritually separated from God. "But God, who is rich in mercy" and love, made you alive and new (vv. 4–5).

What part of us is made new? All of us. Our spirits are made new at salvation (Rom. 8:8–11). Our souls are saved and made new by His Word (James 1:21). Our bodies will be made new when He returns (Phil. 3:20–21). And this is only a taste of what's to come, because "He who sits on the throne" says,

"Behold, I am making all things new" (Rev. 21:5 NASB). His eternal plan is epic, and we get to be a part of it.

You are forgiven of all your sin. Think of all the times you've been beaten down by the wrongs you've done or the many good things you should have done, by all those sins that keep showing up. Could there be any greater relief than to know, in Christ and through His cross, we fully "have redemption, the forgiveness of sins" (Col. 1:14)? Our eternal debts are fully paid. Hear Him clearly cry out, "It is finished" (John 19:30). You are forgiven! By His grace, your record is wiped clean, replaced by His perfect righteousness (Phil. 3:7–9). You've been made free in Christ. And "there is now no condemnation for those in Christ Jesus" (Rom. 8:1). He has conquered the sin in you that was going to destroy and condemn you. All by His grace and for His glory! (Eph. 1:6, 14). He wants you to fully consider yourself now "dead" to that sin and alive to God (Rom. 6:11).

In the next chapter, we'll look at the amazing *inheritance* God gives us in Christ.

But if we are not willing to accept these truths about us, we risk living each day as if we're still lost and unwanted. If we refuse to believe how much we are loved and how completely He has changed and is changing us, we will keep stumbling backward, thinking we are still slaves to sin. We'll be unnecessarily restrained by lies. If we don't discover and keep reminding ourselves of who we are in Christ, we will wander through life still doubting and feeling depressed. We'll define ourselves by our shifting circumstances instead of by God's unchanging Word.

So, on days when you don't *feel* loved and new or accepted and forgiven, look in the mirror and preach the gospel to yourself. Remind your own heart and soul of its truth.

In Christ, you are God's beloved child, forgiven and new.

All these things and so much more are yours, and are enough to leave you with peace and joy for a lifetime!

Father, You have loved me. I praise You for that. You have chosen and adopted me to be Your beloved child. I thank You for that. You have made me a new creation. I don't know how to praise You enough for that. You have forgiven me of all my sin. Help me never stop praising You for that. Open my eyes fully to who I am in You. In Christ's name. Amen.

Going Deeper

Ephesians 1:3–10 • 2 Thessalonians 2:13–17 • 2 Peter 1:3–4

12

Your Inheritance in Christ

What have I received from Him?

"Don't be afraid, little flock, because your Father delights to give you the kingdom." Luke 12:32

Your identity is who you *are* in Christ. Your inheritance is what you *have* in Christ.

This includes many spiritual blessings you can experience *now* and other blessings you'll experience one day in heaven. Our heavenly Father lovingly and lavishly gives all believers spiritual blessings. We don't deserve them, but His grace is glorified through them. The Bible says clearly, He "has blessed us with every spiritual blessing in the heavens in Christ" (Eph. 1:3). These are not empty pleasures but eternal resources that come with our adoption and daily enrich our lives in countless ways.

Let's start with hope. Lasting hope is exclusive to followers of Christ. Hope in this world disappoints. If hope is not anchored in something secure, it's not sure. Our "God of hope" can fill you with joy and peace that's not dependent on worldly circumstances "so that you may overflow with hope by the power of the Holy Spirit" (Rom. 15:13). As the apostle Peter said, "He has given us new birth into a living hope"—that we can enjoy *now*—"and into an inheritance that is imperishable, undefiled, and unfading, kept in heaven for you" (1 Pet. 1:3–4). To be enjoyed later!

So as we unwrap many priceless benefits we've inherited from our Father, try to remember them on the days you feel as though you don't seem to have enough. When you fail or fall, when you feel low or suffer loss, remember these eternal blessings you always have in Christ. You have a rich Father who has lovingly blessed you with true riches (Eph. 1:18).

You have the Holy Spirit. God Himself enters us at salvation. He entered your heart "when you believed" on Christ, and He "sealed" you as a child of God (Eph. 1:13). In ancient times, placing a seal on a document meant the decree or transaction it contained was irrevocable. The Spirit has "sealed" you in this way "for the day of redemption" (Eph. 4:30). He is the guarantee of what's to come as revealed by His ongoing presence. Future salvation is now your "imperishable" inheritance.

But even today, while you wait, the Spirit serves as your internal Helper and Counselor, as your discerner of truth (John 14:16–17). He loves you, bears fruit in you, and enables you to live more faithfully and fruitfully for Christ. He empowers you to do what you otherwise could never do (Mark 13:11; Luke 21:15). The Holy Spirit is your ever-present companion, blessing you from within and making you a blessing. He is the precious and priceless gift of God's abiding presence that you can enjoy and rely on every day.

You have access to God through prayer. Because of what Jesus has done for us, we can now approach the God of the universe, our Father, at any time in any place. Through prayer. Not as unwelcome strangers, but as His beloved children. We now "have boldness and confident access through faith in him" (Eph. 3:12).

After saving us and adopting us, how lonely would we feel if He did not listen to us? But He perfectly hears and deeply cares. Jesus not only prays to the Father for us, but He has bridged the way so we can pray directly to God (John 14:6). There is "one mediator between God and mankind, the man Christ Jesus" (1 Tim. 2:5), who "always lives to intercede" for us (Heb. 7:25). By His blood we are invited to "draw near" to God "in full assurance of faith" (Heb. 10:22). We can approach our loving Father about anything. This enables us to freely pray about everything (Eph. 2:18; Phil. 4:6–7). We can trust that He will hear and He will answer in His patient and perfect timing. Track it and celebrate it!

You have a spiritual family. We tend to view Christian living through an individual lens, but it is not a solo adventure. God is a community within Himself and invites us into community with Him and other believers. We are each members of a "body" (1 Cor. 12:14), the body of Christ, the church. He never intended for us to function alone. We belong to one another as brothers and sisters in Christ and are called to love, support, encourage, and comfort one another.

Paul himself, one of the strongest followers of Christ, openly depended on the prayers and support of other believers. He thrived on the unity they shared as they spread the gospel and made disciples together. We'll have more to say about the church in this book, but it is an essential and priceless element of your inheritance in Christ.

You have unlimited provision. God owns everything and blesses His children with life abundantly in Him (John 10:10). He can supply anything to anyone in any amount at any time. (Phil. 4:19). To worry is to unnecessarily live like an abandoned orphan. As followers of Christ, we have nothing further to worry about. God will always supply somehow. He faithfully delivers.

"Don't worry about your life," Jesus said (Matt. 6:25). That's what unbelievers do. They naturally fret and fear, compare and complain. But not us, not anymore. As believers, though we should willingly work hard and fulfill our responsibilities, we don't need to waste another second thinking our heavenly Father will not supply what we need. He has unlimited power and resources. Our priority is to "seek first the kingdom of God" and walk in "his righteousness," knowing our needs "will be provided" as real-time provisions of His love (Matt. 6:33).

You have a place for you in heaven. Some things about heaven will remain a mystery to us until we get there. It will be infinitely better than any of us could ever imagine (1 Cor. 2:9). Jesus told His disciples He would be going there to "prepare a place for you." And when He returns, He promised to take them to Himself, "so that where I am you may be also" (John 14:3). Though we're temporarily on earth, "our citizenship is in heaven, and we eagerly wait for a Savior from there, the Lord Jesus Christ" (Phil. 3:20).

This is our living hope, a "hope" that "will not disappoint us." How do we know? Because God has already "poured out in our hearts" His love as the first taste of this heavenly inheritance "through the Holy Spirit who was given to us" (Rom. 5:5). Heaven awaits us. It's ours in Christ. So we can embrace this promise from our Father who saved us, fills us, hears us, cares for us, and will never forsake us (Heb. 13:5).

Lord, open our eyes to the glory of our inheritance in Christ and the richness of Your generosity toward us. You are more than we can comprehend or take in. Thank You for Your overwhelming grace and mercy poured out upon us. Thank You for the hope we have in You, for Your Spirit we have inside us, for the access You've given us in prayer, and for our place with You in heaven. May we live forever grateful, forever at peace, and forever in praise of You. In Jesus' name. Amen.

Going Deeper

Psalm 16:5–6 • Ephesians 1:11–14 • Colossians 1:9–12

13

Living Out Your Identity

How should my identity affect how I live?

"Every good tree produces good fruit." Matthew 7:17

What if God asked you to get up tomorrow morning and go pay off all the mortgages and credit card debts of everyone in your city? How would you respond? Likely overwhelmed. Probably filled with confusion, fear, and anxiety. *How, Lord? I don't have the ability or resources. I could never accomplish such an impossible feat!*

That's the way many people respond to the commands of Scripture and to what God asks them to do. After questioning Him, after fumbling and failing, they end up exhausted and defeated.

But imagine if God first said, "Here's a giant checkbook with trillions of dollars in the account. Now go pay off everyone's debt!" How would you respond differently? Less afraid and much more joyful. Excited even! You'd willingly go complete His awesome assignment.

This is what God does for believers in the first three chapters of the New Testament book of Ephesians. Before He asks you to do anything, He reveals the great riches and resources you have in Christ. He says you have a new identity as His beloved child. His full blessings and support. Unconditional love. Complete forgiveness of your sins. The power of the Holy Spirit inside you. A home in heaven waiting for you. Full access to God in prayer. Partnership with the body of Christ. Grace and giftings to accomplish His assignments. His power and presence with you on the journey. Ephesians 1–3 is the "checkbook" you've been given to work with.

Then starting in chapter 4, we learn about our assignments. But because of what we now know about our identity and inheritance in Christ, we don't need to be afraid or overwhelmed by anything He calls us to do. We've already got what we need for all of it, every step of the way.

Follow this pattern. Now that we've been fully forgiven (Eph. 1:7), we are assigned to fully forgive others (Eph. 4:32). Because we are rooted in love (Eph. 3:17), we are called to walk in love towards everyone (Eph. 5:1–2). Knowing God provides, we can stop stealing and start giving (Eph. 4:28). Because He's given grace to us (Eph. 4:7), we can give grace to others (Eph. 4:29). Blessed, we bless. Loved, we love. Served, we serve. *Here's God's checkbook, go share it!* Things we could never do before, we can freely do now through Him.

This understanding should affect how you view all of Scripture. When God's Word commands you to do anything, He's not expecting you to do it by your own power or resources but to fully access His power and resources by faith and in prayer, by the empowerment of His Spirit, not by self-sufficiency. "It is God who is working in you both to will and to work according to his good purpose" (Phil. 2:13).

You now rest and pray, "God, I can't, but You can!" Every believer can now smile at His commands and say, "I can do all things through Christ who strengthens me" (Phil. 4:13 NKJV). The vine will bear fruit through His branches. Christ in you. Christ through you.

So, to let this thinking sink in, Scripture uses the imagery of taking off old, nasty clothes and putting on a new, clean wardrobe that fits your new identity. You are to "take off your former way of life, the old self that is corrupted by deceitful desires" (Eph. 4:22) and "put on the new self, the one created according to God's likeness" (v. 24). You can now pull off old habits and mind-sets that once defined you and put on His new way of walking in the light (Eph. 5:8). By faith. As God's child. Forgiven and loved. Ready to follow.

How should your new identity and inheritance change you according to God's Word?

You should think differently. We are transformed by the renewing of our minds (Rom. 12:2). The way a person "thinks in his heart, so is he" (Prov. 23:7 NKJV). "Therefore," you should no longer live with futile thinking (Eph. 4:17). Empty, foolish, wasteful thoughts were part of our old, dead life. But no more. It's time to grow up and "be renewed in the spirit of your minds" and to "put on the new self" (Eph. 4:23–24). To live "not as unwise people but as wise—making the most of the time, because the days are evil. So don't be foolish, but understand what the Lord's will is" (Eph. 5:15–17). Let's quit thinking we're still slaves to sin, rejected by God, and powerless to do His will. Our salvation is like a helmet that should affect all our thinking. We are new creations in Him! Let's go!

You should talk differently. 'Death and life," the Bible says, "are in the power of the tongue" (Prov. 18:21). Lies, profanity, gossip, and complaining are like rottenness flowing out of a dying and decaying mouth. The tongue may be "a small part of the body" (James 3:5), but it wields enormous power, either for reflecting your identity in Christ or wrecking your testimony. God's Word says, "No foul language should come from your mouth, but only what is good for building up someone in need" (Eph. 4:29). No "shouting and slander" (v. 31). No "obscene and foolish talking or crude joking" (Eph. 5:4). That was us before Christ. But we've been cleansed and renewed now. Our new identity should affect every word we say from here on out. We're to constantly be "speaking the truth in love" (Eph. 4:15). Our lips are to be like fresh fountains of grace, sharing only what is good and helpful to bless those around us.

You should behave differently. When the Holy Spirit came to live in you, He made your "body" His "temple" (1 Cor. 6:19). You are a walking sanctuary. Knowing He is present inside you, how does this awareness impact the way you use your body? Where you go with it? What you do with it? How you take care of it? You now share living space with God's Spirit, who is there to help you experience the beauty and purity of His "holiness," without all the guilt, regret, and damage from "impurity" (1 Thess. 4:7). Unbelievers don't understand the freedom of being purified by God, but you can. Stand up straight, lift your eyes, and walk in honor and purity every day. It's your heritage as His blessed child. You can do this!

You should relate differently. Our new identity should bless all our relationships. His love makes us patient and kind. Once ruthless, now rude-less. It overflows into your marriage, your family, your work, your neighborhood. No more deception. Truth! No more angry outbursts. Patience! No more fussing and fighting. Peace! Aim all your warfare now "against the schemes of the devil" (Eph. 6:11), not against the people God has brought into your life.

On tough and difficult days, Satan will try to make you doubt God's love and goodness, to misunderstand who you are. He'll tell you the opposite of Ephesians 1–3 and say you are not God's blessed and beloved child. When this happens, be strong in the Lord, remember who you are and what you have in Christ. Resist the devil by faith, with the Word and in prayer. Stand in the victory Christ has already won for you. Believe the truth and stand firm by faith!

"Be imitators of God, as dearly loved children" (Eph. 5:1)—not just knowing who you are, not just knowing what you have, but being known by the way your life imitates Christ. In thought, in word, in deed, in life!

Oh, Father, You alone can do these things in me. I offer myself to You today, for You to work Your righteousness in me. Help me to put off those things that have only succeeded at destroying me, and help me to put on the new clothes and full armor of a follower of Christ. I ask in His name. Amen.

Going Deeper

Romans 6:11–13 • Romans 8:5–10 • Galatians 5:24–26

Part IV

Scripture

How Can I Trust and Apply the Word of God?

14

Navigating Through the Bible

What's an Overview of the Bible?

In the beginning was the Word, and the Word was with God, and the Word was God. John 1:1

The Bible is the greatest book of all time. It is the first book ever published and is translated into more languages than any other. With an estimated 5 billion copies in print, it is also the best-selling book in history. It is still the most read and studied, yet most critiqued book of all. The truths it contains have positively influenced the morals of generations and the laws of nations. Many of history's greatest leaders and influencers daily sought the truths of Scripture for understanding, wisdom, and direction.

Every Sunday, hundreds of millions of people around the world still gather to hear the Bible explained and taught. It continues to enlighten and change the hearts of those who believe it. When God opens a person's eyes to realize the Bible is true and reliable, it becomes a powerful source of clarity and comfort. Revelation and inspiration. Healing and hope.

Scripture is like sunlight. It helps us see everything else more clearly in the light of it. It reveals the good and evil in any situation. It honors what is noble and exposes what is sinful. For this reason, the Bible is both deeply loved and greatly hated—depending on the heart of the reader. Truth feels like love to those who love truth, but like hate to those who hate it.

If you receive it, Scripture will befriend you, convict you, comfort you, and then inspire you.

If you keep your physical eyes in the Scriptures, God can use His Word to open your spiritual eyes, clean out your hidden darkness, renew your mind, and set you free (John 8:31–32).

So how should someone approach the Bible? As God's holy Word. How should we view it? As treasure to be cherished. How should we read it? Openly. Humbly. Gratefully.

Here are a few things to keep in mind about how the Bible is designed and laid out:

The Bible is a library. Think of it not as a single book but a sixty-six-volume set. Told through an array of genres, the Bible contains detailed historical records, moral law, beautiful poetry, precise prophecy, and theological letters—each revealing something new about God and how He relates to us. As you study Scripture, you'll experience both the brokenness of mankind and the power and glory of God through remarkable dialogue, intimate worship, spiritual wisdom, and a multilayered display of characters and emotion. This living library is not just for ancient writers to share their hearts but for God to speak directly into your heart and engage with you personally today.

The Bible is a systematic revelation of who God is. God reveals something new and amazing about Himself and about Jesus in each book of the Bible. But He best reveals His relational depth and faithful love through the lens of various covenants He established with His people throughout the generations. The Bible talks about them.

More powerful than a legal contract, a covenant is the strongest commitment in existence. Based upon loyal love, a covenant is established permanently on faithful promises or vows. Covenants are taken very seriously and include great rewards for keeping them, as well as severe consequences for breaking them. Marriage, for example, is a covenant (Mal. 2:14–16).

Like a wedding ring, God provided a sign to reveal each covenant He made. The rainbow was the sign of His covenant with Noah, following the flood (Gen. 9:13–17). Circumcision was the sign of His covenant with Abraham and the nation of Israel (Gen. 17:10–12). When Jesus came, He not only fulfilled the old covenant law but established a new covenant with believers using His own blood. Baptism shows our faith in His death and resurrection (Rom. 6:3–6), and the Lord's Supper is an ongoing reminder of our covenant with Him until He returns (Luke 22:17–20; 1 Cor. 11:23–26).

The Bible is made up of two major parts. The Old Testament and the New Testament. The word *testament* means *covenant*. The Old Testament is comprised of thirty-nine books and includes what happened between God and His people before Jesus came. It tells the story of God's creation, how sin and death entered the world (the Fall), and the covenant God established with one faith-filled person (Abraham), whose descendants became God's chosen people (Israel). God later delivered Israel from slavery in Egypt (the Exodus) and made a covenant with them through the Law of Moses (summarized by the Ten Commandments).

The rest of the Old Testament unfolds the generational accounts of how God continued to reveal His loving compassion and faithfulness to His covenant people. He did exactly what He promised, in provision, deliverance, judgment, and mercy. They were overwhelmingly blessed when they kept His covenant and suffered when they broke it. But when they rebelled, God sent prophets to help call them back to Him so they could avoid judgment or be delivered. At the same time, He was always preparing to send a Messiah who would fulfill prophecy and ultimately rescue His people and all of humanity.

The New Testament begins with Jesus being revealed as the long-awaited Messiah and how everything about Him is superior in every way. It opens with four distinctive historical accounts (the Gospels) of His birth, His life, His death on the cross, and His resurrection from the grave. Like four witnesses in a courtroom, the Gospels present unique perspectives, but they each back one another up.

After Jesus died and rose again, He launched the church. The book of Acts tells its story, how God empowered Christ's first disciples with the Holy Spirit to establish the church in Jerusalem and to take His message—salvation by faith in Jesus alone—to the people of the world.

The rest of the New Testament's books are powerful letters from these early church leaders (mostly Paul) to believers who were becoming known as Christians. It ends with a prophetic message of hope and warning—the book of Revelation—with detailed prophecies of the future, including judgment to God's enemies and life eternal to those who know and follow Christ.

The Bible is all one story. Though it has two parts, it is perfectly united into one whole—the story of God's glory being revealed throughout history and our redemption through Jesus. All the promises and prophecies, all the symbols and sacrifices, are all about Jesus. They point to His perfect life, love, ministry, death, and resurrection that would eliminate the need for ongoing sacrifices. Jesus is concealed in the Old Testament, then revealed in the New Testament. In the Old Testament, *Jesus is coming*. In the Gospels, *Jesus is here*. And the remainder of the New Testament explains why *Jesus came and will come again*.

That's a brief introduction of the great story of the Bible. And yet the telling of it is so rich, and the blessings that come from it are so abundant, that we can drink from it every day and never run dry of new things to learn and experience.

But consider this, how do we know that the Bible is powerful and true? How can a book so old be trusted as authentic and reliable? How do we know it's the Word of God and not just a religious text? We'll answer these questions in the next chapter.

Father, open my eyes and give me understanding of the Scriptures. Open my heart to fully receive its truth. Help me grasp and incorporate the Word of God in my thinking and schedule. Use it to give me revelation, wisdom, understanding, and direction. Make it fresh bread for my soul, meat for my mind, a lamp to my feet, and a light to my path. In Jesus' name. Amen.

Going Deeper

Joshua 1:8 • Psalm 119:33–38 • Hebrews 1:1–2

15

Trusting God's Word

How can I know the Bible is true?

"The one who sent me is true, and what I have heard from him—these things I tell the world." John 8:26

You can absolutely trust the Bible as the Word of God. It is reliable and transformational. And the deeper you dive, the more credible and powerful it will prove to be in your life.

Ask yourself, "Could a perfect God inspire the writing of an accurate book through imperfect people?" If He created the universe, He can do anything.

But what would a book truly inspired by God be like? It would be holy, unique, mind-blowing, and better than all others. Spiritually alive. Solid throughout. Loving but honest. Enlightening but humbling. Awesome yet accessible. Through it, God could explain the design and purpose of everything: where we came from, why we are here, how to live and flourish, and what will happen in the future. It could be relevant to anyone at any time. It could reveal things only God would know and be beautiful, comforting, and life-changing at the same time.

The Bible is and does ALL these things. That's why it has blessed countless lives for centuries. Though skeptics of every generation try to doubt, mock, and attack it, no other book of antiquity comes close to being as monumental and verifiable as the Word of God.

So, what are some specific reasons we know we can trust it?

The Bible is historically accurate. The Scriptures vividly follow real people through real events in real places. Historical records and archaeology destroy the claim that the Bible is fiction. There are now tens of thousands of supporting manuscripts backing it up.

The discovery of the Dead Sea Scrolls in 1948 revealed how faithfully Scripture has been preserved through centuries. The Bible meticulously explains the backgrounds of nations still existent, the fall of cities still in rubble, and the decisions of rulers still carved in stone.

Over twelve wars detailed in the Bible have been confirmed outside the Bible. Thousands of unearthed sites and countless artifacts verify events from Scripture. Among them, there is reliable evidence of our worldwide, common ancestry (Gen. 1–2), a global flood (Gen. 6–9), the destruction of Sodom and Gomorrah (Gen. 19), the exodus of Israel from Egypt (Exod. 12–13), the fallen walls of Jericho (Josh. 6), the burning of Hazor (Josh. 11), the tunnel of King Hezekiah (2 Kings 20:20), the reign of King Nebuchadnezzar (Jer. 39), and the rule of Pontius Pilate (Luke 3:1; 23:1), who crucified Jesus.

You can still visit the valley of Elah where David killed Goliath, Mt. Carmel where Elijah confronted the prophets of Baal,

Bethlehem where Jesus was born, the Jordan River where John baptized Him, the sheep gate where Christ entered Jerusalem, and the Mount of Olives where He prayed and was betrayed.

The Bible is scientifically superior. While science is constantly changing, the Bible remains solid over the centuries. First Peter 1:24–25 says, "The grass withers, and the flower falls, but the word of the Lord endures forever."

The ancient Egyptians believed the earth was held on pillars, Greeks stated it was carried on the back of Atlas, and Hindus claimed it rested on elephants. But the Bible stated God "hangs the earth on nothing" (Job 26:7). We now know the earth is suspended in space exactly as Scripture describes.

Astronomers attempted to count the stars. Hipparchus confirmed 1,022. Centuries later, Ptolemy counted 1,056. After telescopes revealed billions, they only confirmed what Scripture had always said: "The stars of heaven cannot be counted" (Jer. 33:22).

Before satellites, barometers, and electron microscopes, the Scriptures were revealing the water cycle (Job 36:27), the weight of air (Job 28:25), underwater ocean currents (Ps. 8:8), jet streams (Eccles. 1:6), life in human blood (Lev. 17:11), the existence of dinosaurs (Job 40:15–24), and the second law of thermodynamics (Ps. 102:25–26). All these passages were inspired thousands of years before the scientific method had been developed. "For the LORD gives wisdom; from his mouth come knowledge and understanding" (Prov. 2:6).

At a macro level, scientists attempt to observe the universe through time, space, matter, and energy. Yet God's Word introduced this method in the first verses of Genesis. "In the beginning *[time]*, God created *[energy]* the heavens *[space]* and the earth *[matter]*" (vv. 1–2). Solid science doesn't disprove

Scripture. It backs it up. "No wisdom, no understanding, and no counsel will prevail against the LORD" (Prov. 21:30).

The Bible's prophecies are reliable. Hundreds of fulfilled prophecies set the Bible apart from every other book. God puts His reputation on the line with each one, yet He has no difficulty fulfilling them (2 Pet. 1:21).

For example, God promised Abraham, in his old age, that his descendants would become a great nation (Gen. 12:2), live as strangers in a foreign land, be enslaved four hundred years, be freed with many possessions (Gen. 15:13–16), and eventually bless the nations of the world. Every prophecy came true (Acts 7:1–7). The most impressive are the three hundred-plus prophecies made specifically about Jesus in the Old Testament, each fulfilled in His earthly lifetime.

After Jesus walked the earth, more prophecies have been fulfilled, including the destruction of Jerusalem in AD 70 (Luke 21:20–24), the gospel spreading around the world (Matt. 24:14), the resurrection of the nation of Israel in one day (Isa. 66:7–8), and live world news coverage (Rev. 11:9–12). God says His Word "will not return to me empty, but it will accomplish what I please" (Isa. 55:11).

The Bible has unsurpassed unity. The Bible was composed by more than forty authors who were inspired by God, over a span of 1,600 years, on three continents, in three different languages. Yet all sixty-six books form an astounding, united whole, like sixty-six witnesses agreeing in the courtroom of history. All supporting, balancing, and clarifying one another.

For example, the Gospel of Matthew connects the Old Testament from Abraham through David and then to Jesus—all in one lineage of prophecies fulfilled and promises kept. The book of Acts ties the Gospels to the rest of Scripture and explains how the church was birthed from a faithful few to countless thousands. Romans explains the theology of salvation for the entire Bible. Hebrews parallels the Old and New Testaments to reveal that Jesus provided better promises through a better priesthood and sacrifice, through a better covenant. Revelation ties everything together in the world's ultimate judgment and redemption finale while giving clarity, warning, and hope for eternity.

The Bible is simply the most accurate and incomparable book of all time. It's not just true information. It's an epic invitation to know God, be transformed by God, and walk with God in this life and one day in eternity.*

God's Word is a gift to us. And to you! We will discuss how to read, study, and live it out in the next chapters. But know this, you can trust its narrative—God's redemptive plan. You can trust its Savior—Jesus Christ. And you can participate in its goal—the glory of God. As you dive in and live out Scripture, it will radically bless and transform you. And then your world around you. As you devote yourself to it, you will fall in love with it and with the God who inspired it and wants you to experience Him through it.

Lord, thank You for giving me Your living and enduring Word. I praise You that we can build our lives on it and discover the wonder of who You are and who we are in You. Give me a thirst to read it, faith to believe it, and the grace to obey it. Transform me and renew me through Your Word every day, I pray, in Jesus' name. Amen.

Going Deeper

Psalm 19:7–11 • Jeremiah 23:25–29 • 2 Peter 1:16–19

* See page 288 for an inspiring summary of the Bible.

16

GETTING INTO THE BIBLE

HOW DO I READ AND STUDY IT?

"If you continue in my word, you really are my disciples." John 8:31

Studying God's Word is like opening a treasure chest full of gold. The deeper you dive, the more valuable it becomes to you. The best way to think of the Bible is not as a religious text but as loving communication from the One who loves you most. Getting in His Word is your everyday opportunity for knowing God better, growing closer and more intimate with Him. It's not a chore or an academic assignment. It's your perfect Father's love letter to you.

So as you prepare to open the Scripture each day, stop first to talk with Him. Humble your heart before Him.

Open in prayer. Ask the Lord to "open" His Word to you. The psalmist wrote, "Open my eyes so that I may contemplate wondrous things from your instruction" (Ps. 119:18). The Holy Spirit who dwells within you is a teacher. Jesus told His disciples the night before He was taken from them, "The Holy Spirit, whom the Father will send in my name, will teach you all things and remind you everything I have told you" (John 14:26). So invite Him in as your instructor on each day's walk through His Word. He will show you things you'd never see unless He was actively pointing them out to you, causing them to leap off the page to speak to you.

Be very observant. Regardless of whether you're reading from the Old or New Testament—whether it's a historical passage, a teaching passage, a word of prophecy, or a prayer of praise—approach it with an open-hearted curiosity. Ask lots of questions. Who's speaking here? Who's the audience? What's the circumstance? Who are these people in this book and chapter? What is the main point of this text? What is God trying to teach me personally through this?

It helps to know, when reading the Gospels, the purpose behind each author's writing. For example, consider the significance of this: *Matthew* was a Jew, writing to the Jews of his day, seeking to show how Jesus fulfilled Jewish prophecy and was their long-awaited Messiah. *Mark* wrote in the fast-paced, just-the-facts style of the man on the street. He could reach a Roman audience with distilled truth. *Luke,* a physician, interviewed the eyewitnesses and wrote in orderly detail. He checked the sources as an educated and careful historian would do. *John,* whose Gospel is noticeably unique, was more interested in giving an intimate account of what Jesus said, rather than a rolling narrative. As Jesus' beloved friend, John wrote to a universal audience and stated openly his goal: "Jesus performed many other signs in the presence of his disciples that are not written in this book. But these are written so that you may believe that Jesus is the Messiah, the Son of God, and that by believing you may have life in his name" (John 20:30–31).

You'll notice clear differences in how each Gospel presents the life and words of Jesus. The authors had different eyewitness accounts, were writing for different reasons, and highlighted the details that would be the most helpful to their audience. Word-for-word duplication would've meant they collaborated, that they were merely copying from the same source. But when two accounts have different details, it's intentional. *Both* are true. They don't disprove one another, they complement one another. Distinctive accounts actually verify their authenticity and validity, mirroring how we do it in everyday in life.

Interpret in context. The Bible can be misused to say just about anything if you pull random words or verses out and strip them from the context where they were intentionally placed. So look to see what comes before and after them. Check the events and story that's being told around them. Consider the genre or style of writing the writer is using. Is it poetry? A general proverb? A historical record? A prophecy? A summary of events? Every time you read through the Bible, these things will become clearer to you. And it gets very exciting!

Context is always key. If you ran into a theater during the middle of a movie and watched only one minute and then ran out again, it would be hard to understand what's really going on, the bigger picture, and how it all fits together. Likewise, interpreting verses in the context of their chapters, their books, and most importantly the entire Bible will give you the greatest understanding and most balanced and clear interpretation of all.

So try to start your reading at the beginning of books and then work your way through to the end over time. Ask God's Spirit to show you truth through the larger picture of Scripture. Compare passages and let them shed greater light on one another. The Bible is the best commentary on itself. The meanings of words in one book will help you understand their use in other books.

As the Bible is describing an event or recounting lines of dialogue between people, the overarching purpose is not for you to remember every detail. The purpose is to show you something about God and how you can intimately know Him and relate to Him and others. Scripture is a river of truth. You'll never understand everything in every verse, but you can always learn new things and get the fresh spiritual nourishment and direction you need. It is "living and effective . . . able to judge the thoughts and intentions of the heart" (Heb. 4:12). God has given us enough to know Him personally, love Him deeply, and live for Him faithfully.

There are also many wonderful tools that can be helpful in mining the wealth of the Bible: a Bible dictionary (an A–Z list of people, places, and things); a Bible handbook (complete with book and chapter summaries); a Bible concordance (showing places where a particular Hebrew or Greek word appears); a study Bible (which usually includes notes and commentary right there on the page), and more.

You don't have to be a pastor to go deep and fully enjoy God's Word. When you look at Scripture with curiosity, asking questions like a detective on a crime scene, noting key words and details, you are doing the first step that pastor's often use:

observation. Second, when you process what you find in context, then look up cross references, definitions of key words, and the backgrounds of key people, places, or events, you are doing the next step: *interpretation.* When the truth and meaning of a passage becomes clear, then you can do something with it, take responsibility for it, and prayerfully utilize it in life: *application.*

That's why every time you read your Bible, it becomes more meaningful to you—because you're seeking to let it live in you! As you receive God's Word, you're relating with the Author, who is in the room with you, actively leading you to learn of Him and grow closer to Him.

The end result of studying and obeying His Word is a much stronger faith and love for Him, the development of your character into greater Christlikeness, and your greater usefulness in God's kingdom and impact in the world for His glory!

Father, Your Word is a treasure. Please open it every day to me as I open it before You. Help me remember this is You talking to me, not just me reading words. Show me how to make it my lifetime commitment, so that I can know You better and love You more completely. Amen.

Going Deeper

Nehemiah 8:8 • 2 Timothy 3:14–15 • 2 Peter 3:16–17

17

Obeying the Word

How can I apply the Bible to my life?

"My mother and my brothers are those who hear and do the word of God." Luke 8:21

Spiritual maturity can be revealed by how quickly someone obeys God's Word. Scripture will always challenge you to make wise and faith-filled decisions. But will you follow through? The way you choose to respond to what God says is a big deal. It will either change your life for the better or harden your heart even further (Heb. 3:12–15).

Immature Christians are slow to obey Scripture. They doubt and delay. Fear and forget. They rationalize why it's always better to wait and hold back, thinking they must fully understand everything first before they can obey Him. But that's not trust. God doesn't operate that way. He asks us to trust and follow Him *first*, and then He will clarify the path *later*, while we're obeying (Prov. 3:5–6). Anytime we dishonor God, we sadly miss out on the amazing things He desires to do through our faithfulness. Because what good is a command if we disobey it? How helpful is a warning if we don't heed it? God greatly blesses obedience to His Word, rewarding our faith (Heb. 11:6), but He will also lovingly discipline our disobedience (Heb. 12:5–11).

Mature believers take God's Word more seriously. They receive it with humility, faith, and joy. With willingness and wisdom. They don't work on excuses but on ways to make it happen, knowing they can rely on His Spirit and grace to carry them through it. They pray: "Oh, Father, thank You for Your precious Word. I love You and receive it! Please change my heart and life so I will trust You completely and do what You're asking!"

Each of us is accountable and will decide either to walk away from Christ's commands or to take His Word to heart and enjoy the rewards of what He instructs. As we abide in Jesus, He will keep transforming us—our priorities, our attitudes, our schedules, our habits, everything!—until His Word is alive in us. Liberating, transforming, and bearing fruit. Blessing others. Then even when we stumble and fail to obey Him, we can humble ourselves, trust the cross, rest in grace, and get back up and keep growing forward. He is so patient with us. We all need His new mercies every morning!

But in thinking about all this, it's helpful to understand how God's Word works. The following passage shares four key things it does for us:

> All Scripture is inspired by God and is profitable for teaching, for rebuking, for correcting, for training in righteousness, so that the man of God may be complete, equipped for every good work. (2 Tim. 3:16–17)

Each aspect of Scripture is greatly needed to mature us and equip us for the future.

God's Word TEACHES us. Scripture turns on the light of truth so we can see everything more clearly. This type of teaching is doctrine: truth-filled instruction about God, about people, about the world, and how to know Him and the abundant life Jesus offers. Doctrine is not comprised merely of commands to obey but truths to believe. The Bible uses true stories, true testimonies, and truthful teaching to clarify what is reality and what is fantasy, the difference between good and evil. It reveals the true nature of everything. Things get clear in the light of God's Word. We not only discover His nature but our own nature too.

God's Word REBUKES us. Truth helps us realize when we're dead wrong or deceived in some way, when we're walking backwards or living upside down. So some verses will shoot straight with tough love and tell us to wake up, stop, and turn around. To face the insanity and get off at the next exit. The Bible is "a plumb line in his hand" (Amos 7:7), exposing where we're not measuring up—not to condemn or discourage us, but to deliver us from evil and lies, from vanity and stupidity. Even one verse can free up a lot of bondage and baggage in your life. Scripture literally cleans us (John 15:3; Eph. 5:26). If a passage convicts you, don't ignore it, overreact, or get offended. God is love, and He always has your long-term, best interest in mind. He's also worthy of your life and wants to purify you. Therefore, He can do more through you than you could ever imagine (Eph. 3:20).

God's Word CORRECTS us. God turns us from our worst so He can return us to His best. "A command is a lamp, teaching is a light, and corrective discipline is the way to life" (Prov. 6:23). Corrective verses instruct us toward a new, better normal. Toward God's best. They work like a physician setting a broken bone back into perfect alignment. The Bible doesn't merely say to stop lying but shows us what to replace it with—speaking the truth in love (Eph. 4:15–29). His rebuke stops us and His correction restarts us, from walking in bitterness to walking in love and forgiveness. Scripture beautifully shows us His perfect will for the various areas of our lives. Always providing the best way to align us with His nature.

Do you recognize the progression so far? We need *teaching* so we realize what's going on. We need *rebuking* so that we can throw on the brake and the blinker. We need *correcting* to "make straight paths for your feet, so that what is lame may not be dislocated but healed instead" (Heb. 12:13). But there's one more . . .

God's Word TRAINS us. When we get back on track, the Bible helps us stay on track. Jesus doesn't rescue us and then abandon us. He faithfully keeps walking with us and equipping us through His Word for deeper and deeper intimacy with Him and for lasting faithfulness. Many verses give us enduring "training in righteousness" to establish wiser thinking, more reliable relationships, better boundaries, and healthier habits so that we can enjoy all the blessings of freedom and fruitful devotion.

All four of these—*teaching, rebuking, correcting,* and *training*—masterfully work together to clean us, mature us, and complete us. They truly equip us for every good work God may assign.

So when you hear Scripture, how should you apply it? Willingly, joyfully, prayerfully, and intentionally. Doing the Word! Obeying your Lord! Never think of anything He says as being a light suggestion but welcome it as God's holy Word. Eternal truth. Life-changing revelation. Stay in it and on it. Cherish and enjoy it. Pray it and live it—even in small ways.

For "whoever is faithful in very little," Jesus said, will also be "faithful in much" (Luke 16:10). Then you're like the wise person who built his house on the rock instead of the sand (Matt. 7:24, 26). Anchored through obedience. Rock solid in every storm.

Lord, plant Your Word inside me and help me obey it by Your Spirit. Please teach me, rebuke me, correct me, and train me in righteousness. Make me Your devoted disciple, to follow and obey Your living Word, for the sake of Christ and in His name. Amen.

Going Deeper

2 Samuel 22:31–34 • John 14:21 • 1 John 2:3–6

PART V

CHURCH

How Do I Fellowship with Other Believers?

18

THE FAMILY OF GOD

WHAT IS THE PURPOSE OF THE CHURCH?

"I will build my church, and the gates of hell shall not prevail against it." Matthew 16:18 ESV

When we believe the gospel and receive Jesus as our Savior, God the Father adopts us into His family. We are then joined with Christ, His Son, who calls us His "brothers and sisters" (Heb. 2:11). We instantly become part of His global church. His people. His body on earth.

The word *church* itself means "called-out ones." We've been "called" by God out of darkness and into fellowship with Him, along with "all those in every place who call on the name of Jesus Christ our Lord—both their Lord and ours" (1 Cor. 1:2). Every believer in Christ, everywhere in the world, in every generation, is part of His church. It's not a building or a location.

It's not a single institution or denomination. It's not made up of one color, one age group, one kind or caste of people. Everyone who humbly submits to Christ and knows Him is a valued and vital member of His body.

When we believed, God could have taken us straight to heaven. Instead, He intentionally keeps us here where we can grow into a united family together, share our lives in fellowship with one another, and glorify Him with a loving example of unity throughout the world (John 17:21).

Many people do not understand the priceless value of the church. But they would never cut their hand or foot off and separate it from their body. Every member in the body of Christ needs and edifies every other member. People assume they're just fine relating to God alone in private. But the church has many powerful purposes that every believer is meant to participate in, enjoy, contribute toward, and benefit from. Everything we do as the church, we can do better together.

Here are some of the most important ones:

The church worships. Can't we worship alone? Yes, and we should. But corporate worship—all together with one another—is the harmonious and unified way we'll be worshiping in heaven. When two or more are gathered "in my name," Jesus promises He is right there with us (Matt. 18:20). God blesses and inhabits the united praises of His people.

"I will proclaim your name to my brothers and sisters; I will praise you in the assembly" (Ps. 22:22). "I will exalt you *among many people*" (Ps. 35:18, emphasis added). "One generation will declare your works to the next" (Ps. 145:4) . . . "in the assembly of the faithful" (Ps. 149:1). "I will sing praises to you among the nations" (Ps. 108:3). There will be believers from every nation, tribe, and tongue in heaven loving God in worship and loving one another in perfect fellowship.

Not all our worship will sound the same, look the same, feel the same, or be sung the same. But because we "live in harmony with one another, according to Christ Jesus," we can "glorify the God and Father of our Lord Jesus Christ with one mind and one voice" (Rom. 15:5–6).

The church evangelizes. As the resurrected Christ was preparing to return to heaven, He looked to His remaining apostles—who would be the leaders of the New Testament church—and said, "You will receive power when the Holy Spirit has come on you, and you will be my witnesses in Jerusalem, in all Judea and Samaria, and to the ends of the earth" (Acts 1:8). Reaching the lost with the life-changing good news of the gospel is a key priority in the church's job description—a job we do so much better *together* than by ourselves. When the apostles, empowered by the Spirit, put this priority in motion, people came to Christ by the thousands. "Every day the Lord added to their number those who were being saved" (Acts 2:47). Every church should be constantly devoted to sharing the gospel in their communities and beyond!

The church disciples. The Great Commission that Jesus assigned to the church (Matt. 28:19–20) is not just to go and make converts but to go and "make disciples." People who live together in a family don't stay the same age their entire lives. They grow. They change and mature. And in the family of God, we're to "grow in every way into him," into Christ (Eph. 4:15). This is our shared commitment, that we will not merely stand next to one another on Sunday mornings but build up one another during the week, until we all are mature in Christ and able to make disciples of others (Eph. 4:12–13; 2 Tim. 2:2).

The church serves. The church has always been known for being salt and light, for intentionally becoming the hands and feet of Jesus, showing compassion and helping others in the community. And around the world! Scripture says churches are to "devote themselves to good works for pressing needs, so that they will not be unfruitful" (Titus 3:14). Meeting practical needs is an important way, an imperative way, that we clearly model the love of God. It is an extension of our mission to proclaim and model Christ everywhere—in the prisons, in the city streets, in the hurting and hopeless places, anywhere we are led to serve Him by serving them.

The church intercedes. Jesus said, "My house will be called a house of prayer" (Matt. 21:13). Not just the building, but the people. Prayer is a vital and necessary component of everything else the church is called to do. "First of all," Paul said, "I urge that petitions, prayers, intercessions, and thanksgivings be made for everyone" (1 Tim. 2:1). Prayer is the wind in the sails of every ministry. We can do so much good, overcome so much evil, and reach so many who are unreachable—we can do the impossible—if we will first get serious about getting together on our knees and interceding for the souls of men. God answers the prayers of His praying church (Acts 12:5–11). We are to stay "alert with all perseverance and intercession for all the saints" (Eph. 6:18).

First Peter 2 summarizes it well. Who are you, church? "You are a chosen race, a royal priesthood, a holy nation, a people for his possession, so that you may proclaim the praises of the one who called you out of darkness into his marvelous light" (v. 9). The church is, as Jesus said, "the light of the world" (Matt. 5:14). He has "shone in our hearts" (2 Cor. 4:6) so that we can shine His light of truth like a beacon of hope in the darkness.

Why be part of a church then? Because we need one another, have more fun, get more done, and grow more like Jesus through the interaction. When the world sees believers united in fulfilling Christ's mission, they will see Jesus in ways we could never show them by ourselves. Please come join your place in this family. You are more than welcome here. You belong here!

Father, thank You for receiving us into Your family for the sake of Christ, and for putting us together as a family to live out the mission of Christ. Widen my vision for the part You want me to play in helping Your church grow in reach and impact. I ask in Jesus' name. Amen.

Going Deeper

John 17:20–23 • Romans 9:25–26 • Ephesians 4:11–16

19

FAMILY FELLOWSHIP

HOW CAN I GET THE MOST OUT OF CHURCH?

"May they all be one, as you, Father, are in me and I am in you." John 17:21

Living for Jesus has never been a solo sport. Every church that follows Scripture becomes a fertile ecosystem, in which the Christians in that church grow and thrive together. It's a shared journey that God has established for each of us. We hold this living relationship in common. Consequently, the whole experience of being together in the church is meant to be very relational and very cooperative. Unity. Love. Mutual edification. Everyone blessed, and everyone a blessing.

Just as we don't play football alone, or fight wars alone, or play all the instruments in a symphony alone, we need a team, an army, and a unified orchestra if we want to grow effectively and glorify God on the earth. Certain tasks are impossible for us to achieve as individuals. In fact, there are as many as fifty commands in the Bible that we cannot obey if we're trying to follow Christ while separated from His church.

So this is not just a suggestion. The church is essential to our life with Christ. He hasn't created the church to interrupt Sunday plans but to give us united *fellowship*. Being the greatest family and team on earth. Enjoying rich relationships with one another. Sharing joys and sharing sorrows. Sharing needs and sharing resources. Sharing prayer requests and sharing answers. This is not what every church is, but it is biblically what every local church should be.

It's like a *body*. That's how Paul describes the church. "We who are many are one body in Christ and individually members of one another" (Rom. 12:5), "fitted and knit together by every supporting ligament" (Eph. 4:16). We have a head—Jesus—"the head of the body, the church" (Col. 1:18). All believers are members of the body. *The body of Christ*.

A human body is made up of many parts, each of them doing different things, each of them positioned in different places, none of them looking or functioning exactly like other parts of the body. And yet they work together. Their functions interconnect and interrelate with one another. They routinely join forces—arms and hands, eyes and ears—to do more together than either of them can do separately. They take care of one another. The hand wipes the eye. The ears hear danger, then the mind alerts the legs and feet to rush the whole body to safety.

It's this "one another" aspect of the church that we need to embrace and literally embody. Consider the many *"one anothers"* that are clearly stated in Scripture:

"Love one another" (John 13:34). "Welcome one another" (Rom. 15:7). "Instruct one another" (Rom. 15:14). "Greet one another" (1 Cor. 16:20). "Serve one another" (Gal. 5:13). "Be kind and compassionate to one another" (Eph. 4:32). "Bearing with one another and forgiving one another" (Col. 3:13). "Admonishing one another" (Col. 3:16).

"Encourage one another" (1 Thess. 5:11). "Comfort one another" (1 Thess. 4:18 NASB). "Pursue what is good for one another" (1 Thess. 5:15). "Confess your sins to one another and pray for one another" (James 5:16). "Be hospitable to one another" (1 Pet. 4:9).

In other words, as a blessed people who've been given fellowship with the living Christ, "have fellowship with one another" (1 John 1:6–7) in your everyday life.

That's how you get the most out of church. By not just sitting and listening and leaving, but reaching out and getting to know each other on this shared journey of faith in Jesus.

Every time you get together with other believers and spend time together, you are functioning as the church—wherever you're located, however few or many you are (Matt. 18:20). And each time you do, the love of Christ should be pouring out of each of you. Discovering and serving one another's needs. Every member blessing every other member. Even at those times when hard things are needing to be said—which is part of your responsibility as His body, "so that none of you is hardened by sin's deception" (Heb. 3:13)—everything you say should be done for building up and encouraging one another.

You've even been given specific gifts by God for doing this. "If service, use it in service; if teaching, in teaching; if exhorting, in exhortation; giving, with generosity; leading, with diligence; showing mercy, with cheerfulness" (Rom. 12:7–8). No single person or leader is responsible for doing all the work. Instead, every part of the body is vital and valuable.

But maybe you don't feel that way. Maybe you don't think your gifts or your presence is all that necessary for the church to function at full capacity. But "if the foot should say, 'Because I'm not a hand, I don't belong to the body,' it is not for that reason any less a part of the body" (1 Cor. 12:15). Without all the members doing what all the members are gifted and equipped to do, the whole body suffers. We must both *support* one another and *receive* from one another. We "carry one another's burdens," and so we "fulfill the law of Christ" in caring for each other (Gal. 6:2).

It's a beautiful thing.

We're going to be doing this forever in heaven. We won't be divided by denomination or demographic. We'll be worshiping the Lord together and forever enjoying one another. So consider this coming Sunday, and every day in between, your chance to practice. Come to give, come to receive. Come enjoy Christ's body on the earth.

Father, You've drawn us together and invited us into fellowship with one another. Show me where I've been resisting this blessing. Love me through the church and love the church through me. Lead me to the places where I can serve and be blessed. I pray through Christ. Amen.

Going Deeper

1 Corinthians 12:12–27 • Hebrews 10:24–25 •
1 Peter 4:8–11

20

FAMILY IMPERFECTIONS

HOW DO I HANDLE THE BROKENNESS IN THE CHURCH?

"Holy Father, protect them by your name that you have given me, so that they may be one as we are one." John 17:11

We've been talking about God's church as it *can* be and *should* be. In healthy churches, God's Word is preached, God's people are praying, God's presence is felt, God's Spirit is working, God's love is flowing, God's power is evident, God's kingdom is advancing, and God's children are walking in love, joy, grace, and peace.

Being part of a loving, unified body of believers is a taste of heaven. These churches transform their communities. They shine like stars in the universe (Phil. 2:15). This is what happened in Acts, where the church functioned "together" every day of the week, "praising God and enjoying the favor of all the people" (Acts 2:44, 47).

And it's still happening today in many places around the globe. In a perfect world, every church would be like this!

But not all of them are. Some churches look *nothing* like Scripture. They are spiritual dumpster fires! They're distracted, divided, depressed, and basically dead. Not every church is worth joining. Not every so-called spiritual leader is saved and walks with God. Some are wicked deceivers who don't believe, teach, or obey the Bible. They teach their own human philosophies and lead people astray. The Bible warns believers to be on the alert against false teachers who are spiritually unqualified (2 Cor. 11:13–15), who spout heresy, deny the lordship of Jesus, and walk in greed and sin (2 Pet. 2:1–3). We should recognize them and avoid them. God promises to judge them.

Other churches are led by Bible-believing teachers, people who started well, but who have slowly drifted into sin and apathy over time. They were once obedient, but they've quit abiding, they've gotten hurt, they've caved under pressure, or have become distracted in busyness and burned out in ministry. Now they live in constant survival mode. Focusing on themselves. Spiritually depleted.

You do not see many lives changed in these churches—not many prayers answered, not many needs met, not many people saved, baptized, and discipled. They may be busy with religious activities, but they're not showing much evidence of unity, growth, or lasting fruitfulness.

In some places, ungodly people claiming to be spiritual have carried out great amounts of evil and abuse. Unimaginable and unacceptable. Toxic and demonic. It should humble us that any church, if not careful, can get off focus, start coasting into a comfort zone, and drift into apathy or division. Jesus repeatedly confronted and harshly rebuked the scribes and Pharisees of His day for their hypocrisy and poor leadership. He exposed them, called them sons of hell, and strongly warned people about them.

With all this in mind, realize the importance of asking God to guide you to the right church.* But don't expect any church to be a perfect church. You must always keep your eyes on Jesus, not on people. Every congregation is made up of imperfect men and women with imperfect leaders. All from varied backgrounds and in various stages of spiritual maturity. It's what makes the gospel so necessary and beautiful. So transformational!

Not even the church in Acts was free of problems. Like every church, the first church was filled with imperfect people, many of whom brought their own drama into the fellowship. Some of them were lying to each other, covering up their corruptions (Acts 5:1–3), or complaining that the church wasn't doing enough for them (Acts 6:1).

But instead of everyone folding their tents in failure or forsaking the church, they met and worked through each issue together. They kept their eyes on Jesus. They relied on His Spirit. They prioritized prayer and the Word. They didn't bail, they bonded. And as they walked by faith, God kept turning so much bad into so much good for His glory!

This is a great example for us today. It encourages us. This church was full of issues, but God was in it. He powerfully used it and constantly blessed it. We owe the existence of the living churches today around the world to the faithful people of that first church.

We should all be pursuing and enjoying rich fellowship with other believers. But when we are wronged or find ourselves disillusioned by what's happening in our church or by a leader we thought we could trust, it's time to pray, forgive, gather, and speak the truth in love. Not to sulk, sour, and isolate.

In thriving churches, people are willing to seek God together, humble themselves, pray together, walk in His grace and forgiveness, and work through issues by practicing sacrificial love. They constantly pursue what is good, and they hold themselves and their leaders to high standards. They build and guard unity at every level. When evil, division, distractions, or sin show up—and they always will—spiritually mature believers humbly and immediately work together to resolve it (Gal. 6:1), knowing small sparks can become raging fires if not quickly addressed.

How else will we experience the unity that the first church enjoyed unless we're walking in constant grace? Grace saves us and sustains us. It is our lifeblood, helping us to walk in patience, kindness, and forgiveness. Dealing honestly with sin but extending grace throughout the journey toward repentance and restoration. Jesus never ran away from broken people. He loved them and served them as God's beloved Son who was sent to them. But He lovingly exhorted, rebuked, and instructed pastors of sick churches to repent and return to Him as their first love (Rev. 2:4–5). God can resurrect a dead church if the leaders and members will die to themselves and fully surrender to Jesus.

None of the problems in Christ's church are His fault. The "pioneer" of our salvation is eternally "perfect" (Heb. 2:10). He deeply loves and willingly died for His bride. He is purifying her, getting us ready for His return. And we can join Him in this, by staying devoted to His church, by walking with Him intimately and helping others keep doing it as well! We owe Him our highest praise. He never takes His eye off His beloved.

This world desperately needs healthy churches! We must keep planting and building them. Praying for those around us to stay alive and thrive. Never forsaking the assembling of ourselves together with other believers (Heb. 10:25) but joining our Lord in accomplishing His great mission on earth!

Whenever you become discouraged and frustrated by some of what you see taking place in your church or in any church, look to God's Word, where Jesus is seen, standing in the heavens, brilliantly stunning, dazzling in appearance (Rev. 1:12–16). And in His hand, safe in His hand, is His church. Eternally cared for. Eternally protected. Eternally accomplishing what His hand alone is able to do.

Heavenly Father, we ask today that You establish vibrant and living churches in our communities and among the nations. Birth new ones. Heal broken ones. Remove wicked leaders. Raise up godly leaders. You promised You would build Your church. Forgive us, anytime we have acted contrary to Your mission. May we repent and return to You. Purify and unify Your bride! May we serve You faithfully in the fellowship You give us for this kingdom mission. In Jesus' name. Amen.

Going Deeper

1 Corinthians 10:32–33 • Ephesians 3:20–21 •
Revelation 3:11–13

* See page 290 for guidance on how to choose a church.

Part VI

Prayer

How Can I Pray Effectively?

21

Jesus' Example of Prayer

How can I pray effectively?

After dismissing the crowds, he went up on the mountain by himself to pray. Matthew 14:23

Jesus prioritized prayer above almost everything else, which is surprising if you think about it. If anyone didn't seem to need prayer, it would be the Son of God who walked in perfection, who always had the wisdom, knowledge, and power of God with Him.

Why was prayer so important for *Him*?

The answer could tell us why prayer is so important for us.

Prayer, at its heart, is very relational. It's how we communicate and better enjoy our communion with God. While Jesus the Son was here on earth, He was inhabited by God's Spirit, but He was temporarily separated from the glorious presence of His Father in heaven (John 17:11; 20:17). But because He had prayer available to Him, Jesus could constantly talk with Him anywhere at any time about anything. They were in constant fellowship. He *needed* prayer as a man, the same way we need prayer to stay intimately close to our heavenly Father. Constantly in communication with our God. Accessing His grace and guidance, His strength and solace, His provision and protection at any moment.

So while Jesus was modeling prayer to His disciples, demonstrating the imperative of it in His daily life, He was also constantly abiding and depending on it. Modeling the way for us.

What specific examples of prayer did Jesus give us?

He prayed in private. "He often withdrew to deserted places and prayed" (Luke 5:16). Jesus regularly talked in secret to His Father as the only audience. Asking and receiving. Loving and enjoying His Father. Honoring and submitting to Him. Then Jesus would step into the day with boldness, with wisdom and readiness to carry out His Father's perfect will. Rather than playing to the crowds, letting them dictate His schedule, Jesus knew when it was time to dismiss them and retreat into prayer, away from the noise (Mark 6:45–46).

He prayed in public. Though He primarily prayed in private, Jesus sometimes joined the biblical examples of Moses, Joshua, David, Solomon, and Elijah, who prayed boldly before gatherings of people. For example, at the raising of Lazarus from the dead, Jesus intentionally prayed publicly "because of the crowd standing here," so that afterward they would know the Father heard His request and would "believe" He was the Messiah (John 11:42).

Hearing godly people sincerely pray is one helpful way we can learn to pray ourselves. The only problem with public prayer, Jesus warned, is when the motive becomes "to be seen by people" (Matt. 6:5). To impress. To pretend we're more spiritual than we are. Jesus said not to expect an answer to these insincere prayers. Public prayer should be humble and to the point. When you pray in front of others, die to yourself and focus on the Lord of lords, not the people listening. God is your audience, and He is enough.

He prayed BEFORE important events. Before choosing His twelve apostles, Jesus "went out to the mountain to pray and spent all night in prayer to God" (Luke 6:12). He bathed His decisions and ministry in prayer, seeking the Father's will first, preparing for what was to come. It was after praying "well into the night" that He departed to meet up with His disciples on a raging sea, walking on water to rescue them in their storm-tossed boat (Matt. 14:23). He didn't do it to impress them but encourage them, to reveal His true identity to them.

He prayed DURING important events. More than once, after ministering in remote places, Jesus found Himself with thousands of people in need of food. Despite His disciples' insistence that He should send them away, He told them to bring Him what little they could collect. Before miraculously multiplying loaves and fish, Jesus looked "up to heaven, he blessed and broke them," then kept "giving them to the disciples to set before the crowd" (Luke 9:16). Any event could become a prayer event. Talking to the Father. For the glory of the Father.

He prayed AFTER important events. Following His critical last conversation with the disciples in the hours before His death—an incredible, red-letter event that lasted for three chapters in the Bible (John 14–16)—He closed by allowing us behind the veil to hear an intimate conversation with His Father (John 17). He prayed for the Father to "glorify" Him (v. 1), to "protect" them (v. 11), to "sanctify" them by the truth of His word (v. 17). He even prayed for us, those who would "believe in me" through the preaching of His gospel (v. 20).

He prayed in a seamless conversation. He could be "praying in private" one second, then teaching His disciples the next (Luke 9:18). He amazed them with His ability to "pray without ceasing" (1 Thess. 5:17 NASB) as a natural, ongoing rhythm of His life.

And now He makes this kind of praying possible for us. We would not enjoy the privilege of prayer if it weren't for Jesus. But in His name—through His role as our great high priest—"we have boldness to enter the sanctuary through the blood of Jesus" (Heb. 10:19). We can "approach the throne of grace" at every moment, under any conditions as His redeemed children, certain to "receive mercy and find grace to help us in time of need" (Heb. 4:16).

Jesus proved it. And He invites us graciously into this relationship. He says with confidence, "Whatever you ask in my name, I will do it so that the Father may be glorified in the Son" (John 14:13). Pray like Jesus, through Jesus, in the name of Jesus, and you will pray effectively. No doubt about it.

Father, I come to You in the name of Jesus, asking You to make me a person of effective prayer. Help me to follow the example of Jesus. I ask You to grow in me the kind of faith, desire, and boldness that will cause me to walk closely with You in abiding prayer in every season. Through the pure and spotless name of Jesus. Amen.

Going Deeper

Psalm 5:1–7 • Mark 11:22–24 • Hebrews 5:7–9

22

JESUS' MODEL PRAYER

WHAT CAN I LEARN FROM THE LORD'S PRAYER?

"Lord, teach us to pray." Luke 11:1

"He was praying in a certain place, and when he finished," His disciples realized that whatever they thought they knew about prayer, Jesus knew immensely more (Luke 11:1). The priority of it. The intimacy of it. The specificity of it. The obvious power of it.

What a significant moment. Imagine the *knowing delight* on His face, seeing them so curious and open, ready to learn. "You should pray like this," He said (Matt. 6:9). What He shared next would forever impact millions of prayers across the world.

It was a powerful model. Not merely a script. He said to pray "like this." We don't have to pray His exact words in the same order, though there is nothing wrong with that. But this was not a prayer to just mindlessly repeat. And yet so many keys are included in this amazing master class from the master of prayer that we should step in closer and learn from Him.

To learn about prayer, you should focus on learning about God. Who He is. What He can do. What He desires. How to relate to Him. How to speak to Him. This is what Jesus' model prayer shows us.

God is a Father. "Our Father in heaven" (Matt. 6:9). We'll go deeper soon on what it means for God to be our perfect Father, but what a privilege it is to be His child. We begin focusing on God, trusting His revealed nature. Prayer is so much more than saying religious-sounding words. It's always a real conversation in a real relationship. Let it sink in that He can see and hear you and is listening. We come as His children, loved and accepted by Him, the way Jesus is loved and accepted. He's very personal—not just *the* Father, but our Father. Not just *my* Father, but of all those who believe in Him. Jesus expands our thinking to automatically include others as we pray.

God is holy. "Hallowed be Your name" (Matt. 6:9 NASB). Being personal with Him doesn't mean we are peers with Him. He is hallowed. Holy. Set apart and extremely special. Unlike any other. Incomparable. Everything He does is holy. His name is holy. Were it not for the blood of Jesus, we could never approach His awesome presence or speak to Him at all.

What an honor to be invited. Welcomed because of Jesus. And we should never take it lightly. We should always see prayer as sacred. It's good to pause before you begin praying, take in a breath, and remember—He is holy. High and lifted up. Worthy of your highest adoration and greatest respect. Fully able to do anything.

God is King. "Your kingdom come" (Matt. 6:10). He is a King fully reigning in the heavens. "The LORD has established his throne in heaven, and his kingdom rules over all" (Ps. 103:19). In heaven He is worshipped and obeyed constantly. What He desires is and should always be done: "Your will be done." But is His will being done in our lives personally? In our families, churches, and cities? "On earth as it is in heaven" (Matt. 6:10)? In prayer we invite His rule onto our rebel turf. We submit our self-governing hearts to Him. That's how Jesus prayed: "Not my will, but yours, be done" (Luke 22:42). *Come rule in us, rule over us, every day, in every way.* Not just now, but until He comes again.

God is our provider. "Give us today our daily bread" (Matt. 6:11). We should pray daily about whatever we need for that day. We have nothing unless God gives it. And His method of delivery is to faithfully supply what we need every new day. Like the children of Israel in the wilderness, who depended on Him for manna each morning, we come into each day in need of Him. Not just for physical "bread alone" but for "every word that comes from the mouth of God" (Matt. 4:4), from Jesus, "the bread of life" (John 6:35). God has a fresh word from His Word for us every day, and prayer helps us make sure we don't miss it. Ask Him. More than anyone or anything on earth, God is your provider. Jesus told us to ask, believing we'll receive (Mark 11:24). What do you need today? Have you paused and prayed about it?

God is merciful and forgiving. "Forgive us our debts, as we also have forgiven our debtors" (Matt. 6:12). Your gracious God wants you to experience the full joy of knowing your "transgression is forgiven," that your "sin is covered" (Ps. 32:1), that He's driven it away from you "as far as the east is from the west" (Ps. 103:12). In prayer, you can remember and experience it every day. The "abundance" of His mercy, the "refreshing stream" of His forgiveness (Ps. 36:8). It's all yours to enjoy by confessing your sins to Him, by letting them all go. Quickly. Repentantly.

And as we depend on His grace, we freely extend it to others. We let others go too—the people who have hurt or wronged us that we have not forgiven. This is not an either/or proposition. Jesus said it was necessary. By holding others hostage to our grudges, not forgiving them "as God also forgave [us] in Christ" (Eph. 4:32), we are now sinning again ourselves. We are out of fellowship with God. No longer abiding in intimate fellowship with Him. But prayer is where we make it right, by coming before our merciful and forgiving Father. Receiving forgiveness, extending forgiveness. Always. Every day.

God is our protective leader. "Do not lead us into temptation" (Matt. 6:13 NASB). Prayer provides a preemptive strike against future sin. We should come to our all-wise God who already knows every potential snare and tough situation that could threaten the stability of our walk. He can lead us away from it by His Spirit. He can warn us with His Word. He can teach us how to follow His provided way of escape (1 Cor. 10:13 NASB). He wants us walking in faithfulness and fullness. Secure and protected (Ps. 91). Abiding and abundant (John 10:10).

God is our deliverer. "Deliver us from evil" (Matt. 6:13 NASB). Just as He can guard us ahead of time, He can also deliver us from evil in real time. "Your adversary the devil is prowling around like a roaring lion, looking for anyone he can devour" (1 Pet. 5:8). David prayed for deliverance. Moses prayed for deliverance. Esther prayed for deliverance. Daniel prayed for deliverance. And God listened and faithfully rescued each one of them. "The Lord knows how to rescue the godly from trials" (2 Pet. 2:9).

Every new day, new need, and new challenge is a new opportunity to approach our heavenly Father for new grace, new provision, new direction, and new protection. Prayer is not an afterthought; it should be our first thought. And when He is first in our hearts, our prayers become a powerful, effective way to rest in His loving arms and to place all of our lives in His loving hands!

Father in heaven, teach me how to pray. Make me a powerful and effective prayer warrior. Open my eyes to who You are and how I can better know, love, and honor You as my Father. Thank You for inviting me in. May I always approach You in a trusting and respectful way. Strengthen my prayer life and my faith. Help me glorify You with every answer. In Jesus' name. Amen.

Going Deeper

2 Chronicles 6:34–39 • Ephesians 3:14–21 • Jude 24–25

23

Jesus' Teaching on Prayer

What can I ask for when I pray?

"If you abide in Me, and My words abide in you, ask whatever you wish, and it will be done for you." John 15:7 NASB

Prayer is powerful and can accomplish what God can accomplish. Whatever we are facing, prayer can address it. Jesus invites us to pray about anything and everything (John 16:23).

He said, "Ask, and it will be given to you. Seek, and you will find. Knock, and the door will be opened to you. For everyone who asks receives, and the one who seeks finds, and to the one who knocks, the door will be opened" (Matt. 7:7–8).

But most people, instead of praying, tend to worry all night and work all day, as if meeting their needs is entirely up to them. They don't realize that five minutes of prayer can get more done than five days of work. God didn't send His Son to die on the cross, tear down the veil, and give us "boldness and confident access" to His throne in prayer (Eph. 3:12) only to tell us "No!" when we pray. He of course has every right to deny or delay a request. Loving fathers do that for their children sometimes. But our Father's desire is to draw us close, grow our faith, and move us toward a lifestyle of constant prayers that bring His constant answers. That's what Jesus modeled and how He lived.

He explained that when we pray and our Father answers, two very good things happen: our Father is glorified in Jesus (John 14:13) and our joy as His children is made full (John 16:24). When this happens, God is pleased with us and we are pleased with Him.

Jesus is the secret here. We do not ask in *our* name, but His name. We do not come based upon *our* righteousness but Christ's, since we are not righteous. Not by what *we* have done, but through what He's done.

So to pray effectively, we must know Christ first. He is the way to the Father. But then we need to be abiding in Christ. We should get our hearts in right fellowship with Him (no unconfessed sin) and get right with other people (forgiving them). Then we can get busy praying in faith. Presenting whatever requests we have. Then trusting God's heart and His timing with the answers. Sometimes He responds quickly, sometimes He waits days, years, and sometimes decades, but His timing is laser perfect. He is never being slow, but patient (2 Pet. 3:9).

To help us expand our prayers, Jesus gives us a few categories of things we can ask for:

Ask for your needs. Do you regularly pray for what you need? Prayer isn't just a privilege. It is necessary for our necessities. God already knows our needs before we ask, but He wants us to seek Him. This keeps us humble, deepens our walk, and strengthens our faith. Plus, when He meets our needs, He does it in a way that glorifies Him.

Instead of worry, Jesus taught us to pray for anything we need. If you need money or a job, ask. If you need a house, a hotel, or a hospital built in your city, don't be afraid to ask Him. "You do not have because you do not ask" (James 4:2).

God knows all and knows best. He can deny any answer, but we should never let it be because we didn't ask. He will do what He pleases, but He delights to answer our prayers and is greatly glorified through them! What do you need? Ask and keep on asking.

Ask according to God's will. "If we ask anything *according to his will*, he hears us. And if we know that he hears whatever we ask, we know that we have what we have asked of him" (1 John 5:14–15, emphasis added). How can we know we're praying "according to his will"? What does God's Word say His will is? We can always pray in alignment with those things. Ask yourself: What would greatly advance God's kingdom in my situation? What would be really glorifying to Him? What would line up with His Word and His ways? God is already at work to make these things happen. So we can align our prayers with His agendas. Then watch and wait in confidence for Him to amaze us.

Ask for good things. Maybe what you're asking for is not a need, but it may be a really good thing. Jesus said: "If you then, who are evil, know how to give *good gifts* to your children, how much more will your Father in heaven give *good things* to those who ask him?" (Matt. 7:11, emphasis added). We can ask for good things because God is so good. "No good thing will He withhold from those who walk uprightly" (Ps. 84:11 NKJV).

When you're praying for your marriage, family, pastor, or your city, ask: What is the most loving thing I can pray for them? What could God do here that would be overwhelmingly good? Consider this. Hannah didn't *need* a son, but having a son was a good thing, and so God gave her Samuel (1 Sam. 1:27–28). Jesus didn't *need* the fig bush to wither, but it helped Him make a point that built the faith of His disciples (Mark 11:20–25). Start praying for really good things!

Ask for your heart's desire. Jesus said, "If you abide in Me, and My words abide in you, ask whatever you wish, and it will be done for you" (John 15:7 NASB). The phrase "whatever you wish" means your heart's desires. Abiding in Christ is the secret to effective prayer. It can come with somewhat of a blank check. Jesus was sharing an updated version of an ancient promise: "Delight yourself in the LORD; and He will give you the desires of your heart" (Ps. 37:4 NASB).

When God becomes your heart's delight, and His Word is welcome in you, your prayer life starts to escalate to a thrilling level. If the longing of your heart is to say, "What can I do for You, my Father?"—then the delight of His heart becomes, "What can I do for you, My child?" When *He* is your heart's desire, you can ask for *your* heart's desire. This is mind-blowing.

Our gracious heavenly Father "richly provides us with all things to enjoy" (1 Tim. 6:17). He not only makes food necessary and nutritious but delightful and delicious. He not only made the universe functional but beautiful. Our God "is able to do far more abundantly beyond all that we ask or think" (Eph. 3:20 NASB). So let's dream big and ask. Then when He answers, we can celebrate and say, "To him be glory in the church and in Christ Jesus to all generations, forever and ever. Amen" (Eph. 3:21).*

Father, I come to You today in the name of Jesus, asking for what I need, asking for Your will to be done, asking You for good things because You are my good Father. Teach me, Lord, that everything I need is found in You, in abiding in You, in delighting in You. Fill us with joy and be glorified through our powerfully answered prayers, in Jesus' name. Amen.

Going Deeper

1 Kings 3:5–14 • Psalm 20:1–4 • James 4:1–6

* See page 292 for a way to track your prayer requests.

Part VII

Surrender

How Can I Make Christ Lord?

24

FATHER, SON, AND HOLY SPIRIT

WHAT CAN I LEARN FROM THE TRINITY?

He saw the Spirit of God descending like a dove and coming down on him. And a voice from heaven said, "This is my beloved Son, with whom I am well-pleased." Matthew 3:16–17

There is only one true and living God (1 Tim. 2:5). As Moses wrote, "Hear, O Israel! The LORD our God, the LORD is one!" (Deut. 6:4 NKJV). The psalmist sang, "You alone are God" (Ps. 86:10). And God declared through Isaiah, "No god was formed before me, and there will be none after me. I—I am the LORD. Besides me, there is no Savior" (Isa. 43:10–11).

Yet when God reveals His identity to us in Scripture, we discover this "one God" exists as Father, Son, and Holy Spirit—*three* in One. How can this be? How can 1+1+1=1?

This can be mind-shifting for us. It sounds impossible. A deep mystery. All three are distinct, yet divine. All three have all the attributes and nature of God. All three are honored as God, possessing God's power and God's glory. All three *are* God. Yet nowhere in the Bible are the Father, Son, and Holy Spirit described as three Gods. Always one.

But we should not be surprised that God is bigger than our human capacity to comprehend Him. We *need* a God who is bigger than us. Beyond us. Only Satan, the deceiver, would seek to convince us that God must be doubted or denied simply because He cannot be fully understood. Scientists, for example, are baffled that light can function as both a particle and a wave, but that doesn't prevent us from turning on a lamp or enjoying a sunrise. Though our attempts to describe God fall short, it is clear we can still trust Him, love Him, and enjoy a growing relationship with Him.

But the Trinity doesn't only tell us who *God* is. It provides a window to understand who *we* are. He is our Creator. We bear His image. His triune nature models a pattern for us that helps us. The oneness and unity that exists in the Trinity is foundational to our marriages (Gen. 2:24), to Christ's goals for the church (John 17:21), as well as the basics of deep friendships and effective teamwork.

The Trinity is not just some concept in a theological textbook. It's how we personally relate to God and one another. And it is revealed throughout Scripture.

In the first verse of the Bible—"In the beginning God created the heavens and the earth" (Gen. 1:1)—the Hebrew word for God (*Elohim*) is plural, not singular. When God spoke of His intention for creating the first human being, He said it this way: "Let us make man in our image, according to our likeness" (Gen. 1:26). *Us*, not Me. *Our*, not My. This is the God who made us. There's rich revelation here.

There is relationship within the Godhead. Perfect love. Mutual respect, honor, and loving service to one another. The reason we are such relational creatures is not a quantum accident in evolutionary theory. It's because God Himself, the One who created us and made us in His likeness, is relational in His nature. Eternally enjoying His relationships within the Godhead.

We see it in Jesus' baptism, the opening act that inaugurated His earthly ministry. As the Son came up out of the water, "he saw the Spirit of God descending like a dove and coming down on him" (Matt. 3:16). Then almost at once, a voice came booming out of heaven. His Father's voice: "This is my beloved Son, with whom I am well-pleased" (v. 17).

There's the Trinity. We see it when we look at Jesus. We understand now why He so often withdrew to lonely places, long after dark, early in the morning, to pray to His Father, while remaining in fellowship with the Holy Spirit. These were not lonely places; they were meeting places. He was not by Himself. And neither are we. We are always with His Spirit. He never leaves us. And He has invited us to go deeper into an ever-abiding relationship. Sweet fellowship. Loving intimacy.

There is unity within the Godhead. Unity is always God's standard operating procedure. The members of the Trinity are always in sync. We not only see it in creation but in the virgin birth (Luke 1:35) and through the resurrection (Rom. 6:4; 8:11; John 10:17).

Jesus prayed the Father would send the Holy Spirit (John 14:16), who would come and then honor Jesus, who constantly glorified the Father (John 13:31). That's why Jesus could say, "I do not seek my own will, but the will of him who sent me" (John 5:30). The Father, Son, and Spirit are together on everything. As His disciple, you are intentionally baptized in the name of the Father and the Son and the Holy Spirit (Matt. 28:19).

So when Jesus prayed for His disciples to "be one as we are one," to be "made completely one" (John 17:22–23), He was expressing His deep desire for us to experience and reflect the nature of the God who created us and brings us into His family. There's glorious purpose to our unity. It's not just helpful, it's godly and beautiful.

"Behold, how good and how pleasant it is for brothers to live together in unity! . . . For the LORD commanded the blessing there—life forever" (Ps. 133:1, 3 NASB). This is why Paul instructed believers to make "every effort to keep the unity of the Spirit through the bond of peace" (Eph. 4:3). We must build unity, guard unity, pray for unity, and quickly restore unity anytime it is broken. When believers are fighting and divided, it dishonors God and repels people away from God. But when the world sees believers living, serving, and functioning in complete unity and love, God is pleased and people are drawn to know and believe in Jesus (John 17:21).

There's simply no way to manufacture this unity on our own without the Lord's continual help. He is the one who joins us together in His church with "one body and one Spirit . . . one Lord, one faith, one baptism" (Eph. 4:4–5). God's Spirit and God's Word are always moving us toward humility, gentleness, and love—"the perfect bond of unity" (Col. 3:14). Because when we lock our shields and follow the example of the Trinity, people notice. United believers, like united families, are very attractive and reveal the love of Jesus to others.

If you struggle with the Trinity, lay down your mental hoops and focus on Jesus. "The one who has seen me has seen the Father," He said (John 14:9). When Jesus spoke, God was speaking. The way Jesus lived is how God is. "The Son is the radiance of God's glory and the exact expression of his nature" (Heb. 1:3).

If you want to be a follower of God, follow Jesus. Look to Him. Dive into your relationship with Him. There you'll find what all the advanced doctrinal degrees in the world are ultimately designed to convey. God is One. Perfect love.

As you grow in Him, may you "know Christ's love that surpasses knowledge, so that you may be filled with all the fullness of God" (Eph. 3:19).

I praise You, Father, Son, and Holy Spirit—for the wonder of Your greatness, for the vastness of Your wisdom, for the eternal unity You possess. Grow in me, Lord—in us—this same unity of heart, mission, and purpose, that we may glorify You on the earth. May many people be drawn to You through us, our united love, and through Your gospel. In Jesus' name. Amen.

Going Deeper

Psalm 133 • John 14:7–10 • Romans 15:5–6

25

FOLLOWING GOD AS FATHER

WHAT DOES IT MEAN THAT GOD IS MY FATHER?

"Do not call anyone on earth your father, because you have one Father, who is in heaven." Matthew 23:9

Fatherhood on earth comes from the Fatherhood of God. The first person of the Trinity—God the Father—is eternally "Father" by identity and nature. All believers, both men and women, relate to Him as our heavenly Father because that is who He truly is (1 John 3:1).

One of the first words in the Hebrew dictionary (the language of the Old Testament) is the tiny word *ab,* formed by the first two letters in the Hebrew alphabet—the first word a small child is able to say. *Ab* means "father." You hear it in the name *Abraham,* which means "father of a multitude." You hear it in the voice of Jesus, praying in the garden of Gethsemane, "*Abba,* Father!" (Mark 14:36). You hear it from the Holy Spirit, prompting us to cry out "*Abba,* Father!" from our own hearts to God in prayer (Gal. 4:6).

Abba can also mean Daddy. We are all born looking for and longing for a father. This is not a coincidence. We deeply need and desire the love and acceptance of our father.

We are wired by God for God.

This fact does not diminish the priceless role of mothers. Thank God for mothers! But when kids are little, their dad tends to be their hero (Prov. 17:6). They often derive much of their self-concept from him, from what he says and does to them. When children don't get their father's attention or approval, they can spend the rest of their lives trying to fill that void. Or if they're angry at their father, many of their actions can be motivated by that pain, proving him wrong. Whether positive or negative, dads remain a huge focus.

But not only did God put this hunger for a loving father in our hearts, He satisfies it with Himself—by being our *perfect* Father. The ultimate Father.

Even the best earthly fathers are sinful and limited, subject to letting us down. But Jesus said, "Your heavenly Father is perfect" (Matt. 5:48). He is what we've always longed for but never fully had on earth. "Every good and perfect gift is from above, coming down from the Father of lights, who does not change like shifting shadows" (James 1:17). He chose to draw us to Himself by sending His Son to rescue us, to provide us a way home with full access to Him as our Father. "By his own choice, he gave us birth by the word of truth" (James 1:18).

Everything we've ever needed from a father, we can have in God through Christ.

Regardless of what your earthly father was like, Jesus is now your way to your eternal Father (John 14:6). He spoke the words of the Father, did the will of the Father, and perfectly represented the Father (John 14:7–11). Your relationship with God the Father through Jesus is the epitome of eternal life (John 17:3). He is the Father that all our hearts were born crying for, and we still need Him all day every day. We will not be fully settled or satisfied until we are in our Father's arms. And through His Son, we now have Him and can relate to Him daily.

At salvation, our heavenly Father steps in to fulfill all the roles of an earthly father, only perfectly. He does it through His Word, His Spirit, His church, and through our circumstances and relationships. He is actively working all things together for our good, for those who believe in Him (Rom. 8:28–29).

So when you pray to Him as Father and relate to Him as your Father, keep in mind the following Fatherly roles He now fills in your life.

He is your faithful provider. One of God's names, *Jehovah-jireh*, means "The Lord Will Provide" (Gen. 22:14 NASB). Jesus said, "Don't worry about your life, what you will eat or what you will drink, or about your body, what you will wear" (Matt. 6:25), knowing the Father is owner of everything and He will provide (Ps. 50:10). How could Jesus feed thousands with five loaves and two fish? Because He knew the Father always provides. It is never a problem for Him. Physically. Spiritually. Whatever way is needed. Your Father has more than enough to take care of you. Pray to Him in faith knowing He is your faithful provider and can send what you need when you need it. You can trust Him (Phil. 4:19)!

He is your strong protector. Good fathers protect their children. Psalm 91 is a tribute to the protective nature of God, your Father. As you take refuge in Him, you will discover that you do not need to fear evil or harm (Ps. 91:5–6). This is not permission to be foolish, but you can run to Him and rest in Him as your strong protector. Jesus was fully protected by His Father throughout His ministry, allowed to suffer only at specific times by His will and for His glory. Any suffering or physical harm in our lives must first pass through His powerful and loving hands. We should be prayerful and careful, but not fearful!

He is your loving leader. The Father is the leader of the Trinity. He wisely plans and leads with faithful love. Jesus said, "The Father loves the Son and shows him everything he is doing" (John 5:20). He strategically initiates and directs. He "loved the world in this way: He gave his one and only Son, so that everyone who believes in him will not perish but have eternal life" (John 3:16). God has a specific plan and purpose for your life. And it is perfect! When you pray, "Your kingdom come, your will be done" (Matt. 6:10 ESV), you are seeking His leadership. All people need a loving leader! You have that leader now through Christ.

He is your truthful teacher. Good fathers teach (Eph. 6:4). King Solomon wrote, "Listen, my sons, to the instruction of a father, and pay attention so that you may gain understanding" (Prov. 4:1 NASB). That's not just Solomon teaching his son, but God teaching us through His Word. He strategically gives us "the Spirit of truth" (John 14:17) to guide us "into all the truth" (John 16:13). Every day as you read God's Word, as you hear the words of Jesus and are guided by His Spirit, your Father is teaching you (1 John 2:27).

He is your willing helper. The Bible calls Him "the helper of the fatherless," the helper of "the helpless" (Ps. 10:14). "I lift my eyes toward the mountains. Where will my help come from? My help comes from the LORD, the Maker of heaven and earth" (Ps. 121:1–2). All children need their father's help—someone strong to bear their burdens, to lighten their stress, to do what they cannot, and to come alongside when they're struggling. That's why God also supplies the Spirit as your "Helper" (John 14:16, 26 NASB). Your Father knows you can't survive on your own, that you need His continual support. You can lean on Him daily for help.

He is your helpful encourager. We all need daily encouragement and hope (Heb. 3:13). Our Father supplies both. To bless us and remind us of our identity on the front end. To get us back to our feet after we've fallen. To promise us a future and the hope of eternity. The Father was there at the start of Jesus' ministry, saying: "This is my beloved Son, with whom I am well-pleased" (Matt. 3:17). And in the garden, as Jesus was anticipating great suffering, the Father sent "an angel from heaven" to comfort Him (Luke 22:43). He does not give up on us and has promised He will never leave us or forsake us (Heb. 13:5).

He is your compassionate friend. "As a father has compassion on his children, so the LORD has compassion on those who fear him" (Ps. 103:13). He is "the Father of mercies and the God of all comfort" (2 Cor. 1:3). Our friend (John 15:15). Just as there comes a day when little children grow up to become adult friends to their parents, your Father is a friend to you. He loves you and is loyal to you. He has invited you close, welcomed you in, and will forever be the delighting, compassionate Father you've always wanted and needed.

God, *Abba Father*. Your perfect Father.

Dear heavenly Father, I realize I can truly call You "my Father." You are everything I need. Open my eyes to Your love for me and pursuit of me, Your patience and compassion for me. I praise You today because of all You are. Thank You for sending Jesus. Help me daily experience and walk in this loving relationship with You forever. In Jesus' name. Amen.

Going Deeper

Matthew 11:27 • Ephesians 1:5–6 • Philippians 4:19–20

26

Surrendering All to Jesus

What does lordship really mean?

"Why do you call me 'Lord, Lord,' and don't do the things I say?" Luke 6:46

"Jesus Christ is Lord, to the glory of God the Father" (Phil. 2:11). The question is whether we live like it and are truly surrendered to Him as Lord in our personal lives.

The word *Lord* conveys the idea of a master, an owner, a king. The Lord is the boss in charge. The one with the greatest power and authority. The Lord is in the driver's seat and has the final say.

When Jesus was here on earth, He demonstrated His lordship in every situation. He showed He had authority to forgive sins, heal disease, cast out demons, turn water into wine, command the wind and the waves, and even raise Himself from the dead. "All authority has been given to me in heaven and on earth," He said (Matt. 28:18). He is Lord already. But do we live like it?

Salvation is a free gift from God. It cost Jesus everything, but it costs us nothing. He gives it. We receive it. But being His disciple—following Him completely as Lord—requires us to let go of the controls and submit everything to Him. It requires humbling ourselves down to a place of surrender. In every area. For Jesus to lead, we must let Him. For us to follow, we must let go and lay everything on the altar. Holding nothing back.

That's the fundamental requirement for true lordship. Submitting anything and everything. You trust and follow the one who purchased your salvation, and you let Him lead from now on.

Before you assume the cost is too high, consider this: Do you want a God who is only worthy of half your heart? Or your all? Jesus has a perfect track record. He is worthy of it all.

Being all-in for Jesus is the moment you've been waiting for. Surrender brings needed relief and beautiful breakthroughs. Like a prisoner being released, fresh joy rushes into surrendered hearts. In places where you've long been stuck and defeated, Jesus takes over, and new growth starts to happen. Opportunities to serve and share with others begin opening up unexpectedly. Worship used to feel like a chore, a duty. Now it just overflows from your surrendered heart. You wonder why you waited so long, why you ever thought being your own boss was more appealing than this.

No, this is incredible. Like nothing else. When Jesus is your Lord.

There's a simplicity to it. Like when someone gets married, one covenant decision can simultaneously make a million small decisions. After the wedding, you don't have to decide anymore who you're going to live with, be committed to, or share your possessions or children with. Your whole life, all the way down to routine matters, is now shaped by this one holy relationship.

The same is true with lordship. By submitting fully to Christ and placing your life into His hands, countless other decisions become simplified. You don't question anymore if you're going to tell the truth in a situation, or embrace your responsibilities, or keep your promises. Of course you are! Jesus is your Lord now. And you belong to Him.

Should you forgive someone who's hurt you? Should you show compassion to a friend in need? Should you apologize when you've blown it? Should you pray and obey God's Word no matter how you feel? Yes. The answer to all these questions is a simple yes. Because you've already decided. Because Jesus is your Lord.

The old, selfish, sinful, immature child in us that used to run our lives and throw stubborn fits of entitlement has now been put to bed. Our old self is now dead. There's a new Lord and King on the throne of our heart, One who does all things well for our good and His glory.

What He decides, goes. Period. End of discussion.

When we stop and think about who Jesus is, what He's done, and what He can bring into our lives, surrendering to Him is not as tough a call to make. The harder thing is *not* surrendering and trying to "serve two masters" (Matt. 6:24), when every other lord is so far inferior and less reliable than Jesus.

Yet our flesh still resists. We ask endless questions. But no one who's ever surrendered themselves completely to Christ has done it only after all their questions were answered. We can always come up with another question. Like Abraham in the Old Testament, after being told by God to put His trust in Him over where he should live and what he should do, he "believed the LORD" (Gen. 15:6). Then he got up and went. He did exactly as the Lord instructed. He trusted and obeyed. He surrendered.

Sometimes Jesus would use a radical event to open someone's eyes to His power and authority. After He miraculously helped Peter catch a boat-sinking load of fish, for instance, Peter knelt down before Him in awe and said, "Go away from me, Lord, for I am a sinful man!" (Luke 5:8 NASB). After His disciple Thomas, who'd openly doubted whether Jesus had been resurrected, then saw Him alive, he responded by calling Him "my Lord and my God!" (John 20:28). After Jesus confronted Saul of Tarsus in a blinding light on the road to Damascus, Saul fell to the ground and asked, "Who are you, Lord?" (Acts 9:5). In each case, each person immediately recognized Him as "Lord."

Have you ever had a powerful moment with Jesus like that? After the shock and emotion faded from such an encounter, did you start obeying Him? Because obedience is what surrender looks like in real life. That's when we find out whether we've made Him our Lord or not.

Right here, at this center point of this book, we want to be as clear and plain as possible about what following Jesus as Lord truly means. It begins by believing in God, trusting Him and His gospel, placing your faith in what Jesus did on the cross. *Salvation*. Have you done that? Have you received His forgiveness by repenting of your sins? He can never be your Lord unless you've started there with belief.

But then a choice must be made. Every day. Over time. "If anyone wants to follow after me, let him deny himself, take up his cross daily, and follow me" (Luke 9:23). Giving Him total control over your daily life. The big picture and all its individual pieces. All His. All surrendered. *Discipleship.* Are you doing that? Viewing Him not just as Savior but Lord?

As you do, here's how you live it out. Here's the golden question you will start to bring up in every moment: "What does the Lord want me to do in this situation?" Because to a disciple, whatever Jesus wants is all that matters. If you ask, "What do *I* want to do?" or "What do *other people* want me to do?" you could be heading toward a very selfish or sinful decision. If you ask, "What is the path of least resistance?" or "What will make me the most comfortable? The most popular? The most money? The most impressive?" you are on your way to wasting your life in a ditch of passivity or vanity. Jesus blesses obedience. And He gives us lasting joy that is not dependent on our circumstances.

"What does the Lord want me to do?" is the question that overrules them all. If He is Lord, then He decides. And as you ask Him in prayer and seek out His will, He will give clarity to your heart and mind. He will give you peace toward His path (Col. 3:15), guidance from His Word (Ps. 119:105), prompting by His Spirit (Gal. 5:16–25), confirmation through godly counsel, provision at the perfect time, and open doors to make the way. You will be amazed at your Lord. And Christ will be exalted in you because you're trusting Him completely, because you've given Him charge of everything. The one who rules in heaven is also ruling you. This is the mark of a true disciple.

And it is the joy and privilege of following Jesus as Lord.

Jesus, I call on Your name as Lord. I pray You would be honored as Lord in every area of my life. Help me to trust You and open my hands and heart to Your perfect control. Though You already own everything, I give You everything that I have. Build my faith as I let You lead my life. Take over the things I have held back from You. Forgive my pride. Change my heart. Fill me up and use me for Your glory. Be Lord of all I am and all I have. In Your name. Amen.

Going Deeper

Matthew 7:21–23 • 1 Corinthians 8:6 • Revelation 17:14

27

Making Jesus Lord over Relationships

How does a disciple prioritize others?

"If anyone comes to me and does not hate his own father and mother, wife and children, brothers and sisters—yes, and even his own life—he cannot be my disciple." Luke 14:26

One of the guiding hallmarks of the disciple's life is a compassionate, caring love for others. Relationships take on new meaning when you're devoted to Jesus. Once your eyes have been opened to how deeply you've been loved by God, it inspires you with a renewed commitment to treat those around you with more grace, patience, and kindness. To put them above yourself.

But not above your God.

It sounds sweet and sentimental when people say things like: "My wife is everything to me." "My husband is #1 in my life." "My kids are my highest priority." "Family comes first." But what if our allegiance to family, to parents, to children, and to others creates a conflict with our greater allegiance to Christ? What do we do then? Who comes first then?

That's where difficulty comes in. The lordship of Jesus over you will be tested by the people around you.

Jesus warned us it would. "Don't assume," He said, "that I came to bring peace on the earth" (Matt. 10:34)—not when keeping things peaceful with people means turning your back on God. Whenever the price of being accepted by others requires you to choose a path that is disobedient to God and His Word, that's where the disciple feels the "sword" of this devotion (v. 34). That's where loyalty to Jesus can sometimes "turn a man against his father, a daughter against her mother, a daughter-in-law against her mother-in-law," where a person's worst "enemies" could become "the members of his household" (vv. 35–36).

Truth both unites and divides. The truth of the gospel unites us with God and other believers. His message is love—first for God and then for everyone else. But this seemingly harmless message can also stir up division with those who don't know Christ or don't want to follow Him. We are always called to love them, but they may still choose to hate us.

The hope and plan is to walk in truth, serve them well, and win them to Christ, but that's not always what happens because, as Jesus said, "Everyone who does evil hates the light and avoids it, so that his deeds may not be exposed" (John 3:20). When you stop joining in someone's sin, worshiping their idols, following their agendas, or supporting their ungodly lifestyles, they will likely not like the new you. They may hate you for no valid reason. Following Jesus will expose and test your true loyalties.

In some cultures, the stakes are more severe. People who choose Christ are sometimes subject to being disowned by their families, fired from their jobs, divorced by their spouses, hated by their friends, and even arrested and imprisoned. Just for choosing Jesus. Hated for no good reason other than they believed the gospel and fell in love with Christ.

Are you prepared for that?

You cannot let people you love lead you into sin. Love never leads others to sin. But loved ones could tempt you to sin. This is what happened when Adam chose his wife over obeying God in the garden. It's what happened when Sarah influenced Abraham to shortcut the Lord's promise by suggesting he have a child with her handmaiden. It's what happened when Solomon became more attracted to ungodly women than to following the commands of Scripture.

Whether it's your spouse or best friend, whether it's a demand one of your children is making, whether it's an unethical expectation placed on you by your boss or your parents—if they are demanding that you must do what they want regardless of what God says, you cannot let your feelings or loyalty to them derail you from following Christ. People mean well, but they think selfishly and short-term. Jesus always has your best interest for eternity in mind.

You cannot look to people as your source of value. People are fickle but can be very influential. Part of the tension we feel in conflict is that we inherently want others to be happy with us. We love their affirmation and we fear their disapproval. Moses knew all about this and was forced to choose between loyalties. "When he had grown up," the Bible says, he "refused to be called the son of Pharaoh's daughter and chose to suffer with the people of God rather than to enjoy the fleeting pleasure of sin" (Heb. 11:24–25). Moses had friends and family who praised him one day and turned on him the next. He learned it was much better to please a faithful God than unfaithful people.

Jesus said it this way: "The one who loves a father or mother more than me" or "a son or daughter more than me is not worthy of me" (Matt. 10:37). Our worth and value come from God our Father, through Christ. Loving others more than ourselves is honorable, of course (Phil. 2:3), but pleasing *Him* is vitally more important than pleasing *them*.

You can love them in an even better way. The truth is, to love Christ first is the way you love others the best. To put people first is to love them less. Since God is the source of unconditional love, and because He pours this love into your heart by the Holy Spirit, His love flows most freely through you when you're fully aligned with Him.

So if your spouse is not following the Lord, the best way to love them and lead them to Christ is not by succumbing to their every wish but by being a godly, humble, loving example to them "without a word," by letting them witness your Christlike, respectful, "reverent" life (1 Pet. 3:1–2). Putting Christ first can be an eye-opening witness to curious nonbelievers. Many people have won their friends, spouses, and relatives to Christ over time by walking in integrity and love around them on a consistent basis. The positive transformation Jesus can bring is undeniable.

"The Lord's servant must not quarrel, but must be gentle to everyone, able to teach, and patient, instructing his opponents with gentleness. Perhaps God will grant them repentance leading them to the knowledge of the truth. Then they may come to their senses and escape the trap of the devil" (2 Tim. 2:24–26).

Could they still reject you, complain to you, and pull away from you? Of course. But "your faith and hope are in God" (1 Pet. 1:21–22). You don't take anything good away from them by loving Jesus more than them. You're now loving them with the greater love of God.

And great will be your reward in heaven.

Father, You are worthy of my life. Your call is radical and extreme, yet true and loving. In all the places where honoring You as Lord means I must sometimes feel the sword of another's rejection, I ask for patience and peace, strength and endurance to maintain my love and devotion. Love my friends and my enemies through me. Draw the people closest to me to Christ through the example of my life. Remind me that I love people best by loving You first. In Jesus' name. Amen.

Going Deeper

Genesis 22:12 • John 15:18–21 • 1 John 4:15–19

28

Making Jesus Lord over Self

What is the cost of discipleship?

"If anyone wants to come after Me, he must deny himself, take up his cross daily, and follow Me." Luke 9:23 NASB

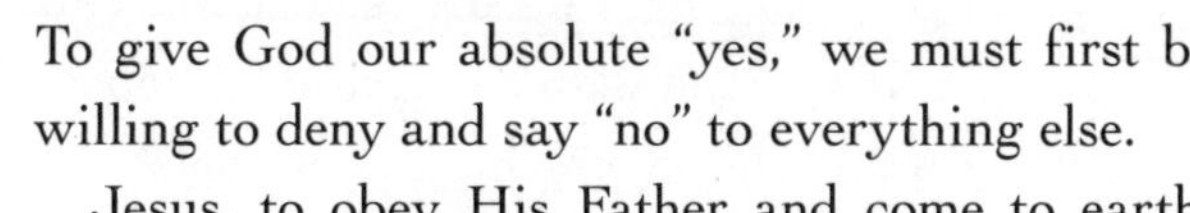

To give God our absolute "yes," we must first be willing to deny and say "no" to everything else.

Jesus, to obey His Father and come to earth, chose to deny Himself and leave behind the joys and pleasures of heaven. To live a life of compassionate service, He chose to deny Himself the right to be served. To save us from our sins and give us eternal life, He chose to deny Himself, praying, "Not my will, but yours, be done" (Luke 22:42). He was then "obedient to the point of death—even to death on a cross" (Phil. 2:8).

What was His reward for all this self-denial? "God highly exalted him and gave him the name that is above every name" (Phil. 2:9). He now reigns in the heavens and is Lord of all (v. 11)! This, friend, is what's called getting an eternal return on a worldly investment.

So now, with eternity in mind, with the reality of His example in view, Jesus says to us what He said to His first disciples: "If anyone wants to come after Me, he must deny himself, take up his cross daily, and follow Me" (Luke 9:23 NASB). In order to say yes to God and pursue what matters in His kingdom, we must first say no to ourselves in this short life.

On its face, it may seem like a losing proposition. *Denying ourselves* means disregarding what we want, saying no to it. *Taking up our cross* means dying to things. Things we have or want to have. Things we value and cherish in this life. Temporary things. It could be anything.

But don't expect to feel cheated or deprived by this decision. That's not what the life of Jesus ever bears out, nor is it the testimony of His followers throughout history who accepted His challenge. Every time we die to something for the sake of Christ, He fills the void with something far superior.

Peter gave up his work, his fishing nets, only to become an incredible fisherman for eternal souls. Matthew died to his business of calculating and recording Roman taxes, but today the Gospel he wrote is read by millions, in more than 3,000 languages. No one reads his old tax ledgers anymore! Paul walked away from his reputation as a rising religious superstar, admitting later that "the surpassing value of knowing Christ Jesus my Lord" was completely worth the sacrifice. Everything was worth giving up, he said, "so that I may gain Christ" (Phil. 3:8).

So it's a *winning* proposition, this dying to ourselves to follow Him. Here, in fact, is the losing proposition: "Whoever wants to save his life will lose it." That's the truth of the gospel. Only the one who "loses his life because of me will save it" (Luke 9:24). Dying to self prepares us for godliness. We say no to selfishness to walk in love. No to lying to speak the truth. No to greed to enjoy contentment. No to bitterness to walk in forgiveness. No to our own control and agenda, to follow His good, pleasing, and perfect will for our lives.

If you want to prepare to live faithfully as His disciple, then first prepare to die. You die to live.

What are we to die to?

Die to sin. Just as you once were separated from God, now through Christ you are separated from sin. Where you once were dead *in* your sins, now you are dead *to* your sins. They have no more control over you, spiritually speaking, than if you were physically dead. But it's up to you, by abiding in Christ, to live in this reality, to daily "consider yourselves dead to sin and alive to God in Christ Jesus" (Rom. 6:11). It will still come knocking, but you no longer answer the door.

Die to selfish desires. Dead people don't get offended. They don't complain. They don't hold grudges. If a dead man was lying on the floor and a beautiful woman walked by, he wouldn't look up and lust after her. If someone claimed credit for something he'd done, he wouldn't stand up and demand the glory. By dying to ourselves, we quit responding selfishly.

"One died for all, and therefore all died . . . so that those who live should no longer live for themselves" (2 Cor. 5:14–15). By dying to your selfish desires, He gives you far better desires. It's an excellent exchange.

Die to self-centeredness. If there's one thing we all should know about ourselves by now, it's that our natural inclination is to focus on ourselves as the center of our world. But we did not create God for us; God created us for Him. We are a small thing to live for. But nothing is greater than God. So let's join those around His throne, saying, "You are worthy, O Lord, to receive glory and honor and power" (Rev. 4:11 NKJV). *You,* not us. "Do nothing out of selfish ambition or conceit" (Phil. 2:3). Nothing. Does our selfish ambition really satisfy us? Does it draw people to Christ? Does it make us more loving and likable? No. Our lovingkindness and humility are what people need to see, but this requires us first to die.

Die to your rights. When Jesus embraced the role of a servant, He gave up His rights so He could serve His Father. Some people will miss heaven because they demanded their own rights and privileges instead of following Him (Luke 14:16–24). Our rights are important, but following Christ, loving others, and spreading the gospel are much more important.

It's all tied to ownership. If you were to make something, buy something, or have something given to you, you would own it. That's why Jesus owns you. As your Creator, He made you. He bought you "at a price" (1 Cor. 6:20), and His Father gave you to Him for His safekeeping forever (John 6:37). You belong to Him. Your right to demand your rights became His right. He now has final say.

So deny yourself. Die to yourself. And take up your cross. If you're to put God first and love Him with your whole heart, you must be willing to let go of anything you love more than Him: your sins, your selfish desires, your self-centeredness, your own rights.

But what else? Do a little inventory. What's standing in the way of your relationship with Christ or your full obedience to Christ? What idol do you treasure more than you treasure Him? What person or place or thing or activity do you habitually keep choosing over God? It may even be a good thing, not sinful at all, but is it eating up all your time and holding you back from being all-in for Christ? Do you want to follow Christ and love Him most? Then you must be willing to lay it on the altar and deny it for Him.

Talk to God about it in prayer and ask Him for wisdom and strength. He loves you deeply and wants you to show how much you love Him. Your eternal gain will be so much more than any short-term loss. You can trust Him on this. On everything!

Father, prepare my heart and life to give You my "yes." You are making me Your disciple. Now show me where I'm not surrendering. Reveal the things in my life that I need to deny, die to, or let go of, even if only for a season so that I can more fully follow You. Then give me the faith, strength, and courage by Your Spirit to lay it all down—anything that's holding me back—so I can experience the joy of knowing and loving You more. In Christ. Amen.

Going Deeper

Matthew 13:44–46 • Philippians 3:14–20 • 1 John 2:15–17

29

Making Jesus Lord over Possessions

How does a disciple handle money?

"Every one of you who does not renounce all his possessions cannot be my disciple." Luke 14:33

If you had to choose, would you rather be very rich or very happy? Would you prefer to be rich in possessions or rich in faith? If you acquired a great deal of money, how do you think it would affect your heart? What would you do with it? Here's a better question: What would a totally surrendered follower of Jesus do with it, someone who loves Jesus more than anything?

The Gospel of Luke records two remarkable stories about two very wealthy men who both encountered Jesus.

The first is known by the description—a rich, young "ruler" (Luke 18:18). He was loaded, prominent, impressively religious, and a moral, model citizen. He ran up to Jesus and asked for something we all want: eternal life. But Jesus answered his request by first exposing a hidden idol in his heart: his money.

Jesus did not tell everyone He met to "sell all you have and distribute it to the poor," but He did to this man (Luke 18:22). He didn't say it out of condemnation, but genuine "love" (Mark 10:21). Jesus saw past the man's luxury to the spiritual poverty in his heart, offering him the perfect advice both to set him free from bondage and to transform his life for eternity. By giving away the extra possessions enslaving him, this young man could not only enjoy fresh liberty and the joy of generosity, but he could store up greater, lasting "treasure in heaven" (Luke 18:22). Plus, the greatest prize of all—the invitation from Jesus to "come, follow me" would allow him to experience the friendship of a lifetime, to have a closer walk with God than he ever imagined. He could quickly upgrade his portfolio—from temporary to eternal riches—while also enjoying Christ's gift of eternal life. What did the man do?

He was shortsighted, faithless, and foolish, so he walked away "extremely sad, because he was very rich" (Luke 18:23). Refusing to follow Christ's invitation, he clung to dead finances over true riches and apparently missed an abundant eternity he could have enjoyed with Jesus.

One chapter later, in Luke 19, in the Middle Eastern city of Jericho, another rich man came curiously looking for Jesus. Zacchaeus was a "chief tax collector" (v. 2), employed by the occupying Roman government. He'd apparently indulged in the common, greedy practice of overcharging for taxes and pocketing the difference. So he was not only highly rich but a lowly cheat.

Enter Jesus, who walked up and surprised Zacchaeus, calling him by name and then inviting himself over for the afternoon. To see Jesus' willingness to visit the home of a crooked businessman shocked everyone watching. At the same time, sudden conviction fell onto the tax collector's heart. Moved by the graciousness of Jesus, Zacchaeus quickly volunteered—without being asked—to "give half of [his] possessions to the poor." And as additional proof of his rapid repentance, he said, "If I have extorted anything from anyone, I'll pay back four times as much" (Luke 19:8)—far more than the Old Testament law prescribed for retribution (Num. 5:7). Filled with joy and gladness, Zacchaeus walked home with Jesus. Choosing wisely. Forever changed.

Two wealthy men, two surprising responses. But what were the key differences between the rich, young ruler and the rich, old tax collector?

The first called Jesus a "good teacher" (Luke 18:18) and stubbornly walked away sad with an empty soul.

Zacchaeus called Jesus "Lord" (Luke 19:8) and ended up filled with joy, forgiveness, and a changed life.

When Jesus is Lord of your possessions, it liberates your heart and how you view it all, starting with the fact that it's not actually yours, that it's always been His. God owns the universe, including every person, plot of land, and every penny. Anything you have is His temporary loan from the goodness of His hand, intended for you to enjoy and wisely steward in a way that honors Him, meets needs, blesses others, and supports His kingdom (1 Tim. 6:17–19; 2 Cor. 9:10–15).

To the sold-out disciple, money becomes a great tool of faith, love, and good works—a treasure not to be squandered on earth but strategically invested in eternity. "For where your treasure is, there your heart will be also" (Matt. 6:21).

This doesn't mean wealth is evil. Wealth can be a fountain of blessing. But it can also have an insidious pull that drains your focus, increases your worry, poisons your motives, and weakens your tendency to walk by faith. Richer people tend to possess weaker faith (James 2:5–7). This explains why Jesus looked at the rich young ruler and said, "How hard it is for those who have wealth to enter the kingdom of God!" (Luke 18:24). "No one can serve two masters," He said. "You cannot serve both God and money" (Matt. 6:24). You can be devoted to only one.

The disciple Matthew followed Jesus instead of money, while Judas betrayed Jesus for money. We will either be stewards or slaves of it. So beware of your possessions possessing you, since "the love of money is a root of all kinds of evil" (1 Tim. 6:10).

Money can be a terrific servant, but always proves a terrible master. Every time we tithe, give offerings, share our homes, and surrender our lives in prayer to the Lord's guidance, it keeps our hearts more devoted to Jesus and less devoted to wealth. We should keep placing our possessions into the Master's hands rather than cherishing it like a lover, wasting it like a fool, or hoarding it like a slave.

What's that in your hand, Moses? A shepherd's staff. When entrusted to the Lord, it becomes the rod of God and helps part the Red Sea. *What's that in your hand, David?* A sling. Given to God, it kills a giant and helps win a great battle. *What's that in your hand, little boy?* Five loaves and two fish. Given to Jesus, it feeds more than five thousand people and strengthens the faith of millions. *What's that in your hand, Mary?* A jar of perfume. Yet poured out as an offering, it anoints the body of Christ for burial and then accompanies the gospel around the world.

Jesus is absolutely worthy of our all. He systematically exposes the idols of our hearts and confronts anything that might hinder us from fully loving and following Him. Just as He left the pleasures of heaven to come to earth for our sake, He invites us to open our hands and hearts to experience the fulfillment of turning everything over to His control so that we might gain vast treasures in heaven. "Though he was rich, for your sake he became poor, so that by his poverty you might become rich" (2 Cor. 8:9). Rich in all that matters.

So, what's in *your* hands?

Lord Jesus, please be Lord over my possessions and my heart. Help me walk by faith and fully honor You with everything I have or own. Remove anything that keeps me from fully following You, and use whatever is in my hands for Your glory. Bless me and make me a joyful giver and fountain of generosity to others. In Your precious name. Amen.

Going Deeper

Matthew 19:23–26 • 1 Timothy 6:17–19 • Hebrews 13:5–6

30

RELYING ON THE HOLY SPIRIT

WHO IS HE AND WHAT DOES HE DO?

"The one who believes in me, as the Scripture has said, will have streams of living water flow from deep within him." He said this about the Spirit. John 7:38

What did great preachers like John Wesley, Charles Spurgeon, and Billy Graham have in common? They were three of the most fruitful evangelists and servants for Christ in the last three hundred years.

God saved all three of them, called them into ministry, and blessed them greatly by His grace. They each served God faithfully for decades, and their spiritual legacies and influence are still bearing a lasting impact today. But each of them specifically referenced their belief in and reliance upon the Holy Spirit as the key power behind their walk with God, the effectiveness of their preaching, and the fruitfulness of their ministry.

Many churches around the world believe that Jesus Christ is Lord, that salvation comes by grace through faith, and that the Bible is the true, living Word of God. But the Holy Spirit is not something they feel comfortable talking about or discussing. Teaching about the Holy Spirit, they think, could lead to confusion. Things could get out of hand. They've heard stories of believers seemingly losing control or behaving disorderly while claiming they were led by the Spirit. Others argue it leads to mere emotionalism or might even be evil. Some churches have split or changed denominations over the disagreement. So in an effort to avoid extremes and keep people unified and comfortable, they've swung to the other extreme and have minimized the emphasis they place on the Holy Spirit.

But we cannot truly follow Jesus' teaching or example as His disciple without discussing the vital role of the Holy Spirit in the life of a believer.

Jesus was blessed by the Holy Spirit (John 1:32), filled with and led by the Holy Spirit (Luke 4:1), empowered by the Holy Spirit (Luke 4:14), and did all of His ministry through the Holy Spirit (Luke 4:18). He went on to talk often about the Holy Spirit's vital and ongoing role in the lives of all those who would believe in Him.

As we've discussed in previous chapters, when we believe the gospel, we are "sealed with the promised Holy Spirit" (Eph. 1:13). We are also commanded not to "grieve" the Spirit with sin in our lives (Eph. 4:30–31), but to be "filled" with the Holy Spirit (Eph. 5:18) and led by the Holy Spirit. What does the Bible say about the Holy Spirit's role in our lives?

The Holy Spirit saves us. "No one can say, 'Jesus is Lord,' except by the Holy Spirit" (1 Cor. 12:3). The Father "draws" us (John 6:44), the Son provides the "way" for us (John 14:6), but our salvation is not complete without "the washing of regeneration and renewal by the Holy Spirit" (Titus 3:5). Jesus said, "It is the Spirit who gives life" (John 6:63 NASB).

The Holy Spirit satisfies us. Love, joy, and peace are lasting fruits from the Holy Spirit (Gal. 5:22–25). But worldly pleasures provide none of those. Part of the allure of sin is the lie that it will somehow satisfy our cravings and be worth the brief satisfaction it gives. Yet we all know the shame and guilt it leaves behind, how it ends in lasting consequences and painful regret. In contrast, Jesus repeatedly referenced the Holy Spirit as His gift to believers, specifically for the task of satisfying them from the "thirsty" experience of this life (John 4:13–14; 7:37–39).

The Holy Spirit helps us. He is our "Helper" (John 14:16 NASB)—our Comforter and Counselor. Jesus said the Spirit was "another" Helper, meaning He readily provides the same help spiritually that Jesus gave to His disciples when He was with them physically. The Spirit is equally God, equally powerful, and He is ever-present within all true believers in Jesus.

The Holy Spirit teaches us. One aspect of the help He gives is to "teach you all things" and "remind you of everything" that you've read and learned about in God's Word (John 14:26). Have you ever had a specific verse or truth from Scripture download into your head at the perfect time to guide your thinking, your praying, or your conversation with others? That's one part of the work of the Holy Spirit, revealing truth to you not only as you read the Bible, but reminding you of it as you go about each day.

The Holy Spirit empowers us. As Jesus was preparing to return to the Father after His resurrection, He told His followers, "You will receive power when the Holy Spirit has come on you, and you will be my witnesses in Jerusalem, in all Judea and Samaria, and to the ends of the earth" (Acts 1:8). Religion teaches us just to try harder and be more committed. But Christianity says to repent, surrender to Christ, and rely on God's Spirit to empower you. We need His power, not just more willpower. No one can bear lasting spiritual fruit apart from the Spirit's work.

The Holy Spirit guides us. The Holy Spirit does not replace or negate the Word of God. He aligns us with it and guides us into obeying it. Jesus said, "He will guide you into all the truth" (John 16:13 NASB). We know He performs this guiding task for us because He not only did it for Jesus and the apostles but also for common believers who walked with the Lord. To the leaders of the early church, after they'd fasted and prayed, the Spirit guided them to "set apart for me Barnabas and Saul for the work to which I have called them" (Acts 13:2). He led Philip's evangelism of the eunuch (Acts 8:29), Ananias's baptism of Saul (Acts 9:10–17), Stephen's ministry as a deacon (Acts 6:5), and Paul's specific route in his missionary travels (Acts 16:6–7).

We do not have to obey the Scriptures in our own energy. We *can't* do it. But as we abide in Christ, we can rely upon His Spirit within us to help us do the will and work of the Lord each day. He will never lead us to disobey the Word of God but only empower us to obey it better.

"Who of you is in any way acquainted with the work of his Spirit?" John Wesley once said. "Can you bear, unless now and then in a church, any talk of the Holy Ghost?" If not, then "in the name of the Lord God Almighty, I ask, what religion are you of?"[1]

"Value above all things the Holy Spirit," Charles Spurgeon would later say. "Without the Spirit of God we can do nothing. We are as ships without wind or chariots without steeds; like branches without sap, we are withered; like coals without fire, we are useless."[2]

"Billy Graham cannot live the Christian life," the world-famous evangelist said of himself. "I've tried. I can't do it. But with the help of the Word of God and the help of the Holy Spirit, I can live the Christian life. He lives it through me."[3]

Through all of us. When we rely on the Spirit.

Father, thank You for promising to meet our needs, strengthen us, and never leave us. Through Your Holy Spirit, You have kept Your promises. As I follow the example of Jesus, I ask that You fill and guide me by Your Holy Spirit. Help me, teach me, satisfy me, and empower me through Your Spirit's power to abide in Christ and do the will of my Father. In Jesus' name. Amen.

Going Deeper

Zechariah 4:6 • Acts 10:19–20 • Ephesians 3:16

1. John Wesley, *Scriptural Christianity: A Sermon Preached August 24, 1744* (London: G. Whitfield, 1797), 23.
2. C. H. Spurgeon, *The Metropolitan Tabernacle Pulpit: Sermons, Preached and Revised During the Year 1874*, Volume 20 (London: Passmore & Alabaster, 1875), 16.
3. Spoken by Billy Graham during a crusade in Portland, Oregon, in 1993; https://www.billygraham.ca/100-quotes-from-billy-graham/.

31

Being Led by the Spirit

How do I follow His lead?

"My sheep hear my voice, I know them, and they follow me." John 10:27

The Holy Spirit is always in perfect alignment with God's Word. He will never lead you to do anything that is sinful or contrary to the Scriptures. Instead, He prompts us as believers to take practical steps that help us more completely follow God's Word. We desperately need His help. We cannot fully obey without the ongoing help of the Spirit.

He is the hand; we are the glove. That's why all believers are instructed to ask for, rely upon, be filled with, and be led by the Holy Spirit (Luke 11:13; Eph. 5:18).

The Bible says we can either "walk by the Spirit" or we can "carry out the desire of the flesh"—one or the other—because "these are opposed to each other" (Gal. 5:16–17). Like oil and water. Light and darkness. They run in opposite directions. Our flesh—our natural, sinful self-centeredness—is opposed to God's Spirit and will lead us away from where Jesus wants us to go. But the Holy Spirit in us will faithfully lead us toward abiding in Christ, walking in love, and following God's Word to the very place He has for us. To truth. To power. To freedom. To effectiveness. To genuine satisfaction in Christ.

But how do we walk this way? How do we let Him lead us this way? What does Scripture clearly instruct us regarding our relationship with and submission to the Holy Spirit?

Be saved and be baptized. Let's start at the beginning. "Repent and be baptized, each of you, in the name of Jesus Christ for the forgiveness of your sins, and you will receive the gift of the Holy Spirit" (Acts 2:38). Anyone's journey to being led by the Spirit begins by believing the gospel. He enters us and seals us at salvation (Eph. 1:13). When we simply believe!

But it's hard to talk about the Holy Spirit and completely ignore the importance of baptism. Not only did the Spirit show up and bless Jesus at His baptism, but believers are intentionally baptized in the name of the Father, the Son, and *the Holy Spirit* (Matt. 28:19). Being led by God's Spirit always includes our submission to His Word. So if we want to walk daily by the Spirit and not our flesh, we must recognize that resistance and disobedience regarding baptism would equate to us following our flesh. It would grieve the Holy Spirit. It does not align us with His moment-by-moment leadership.

Be repentant. Sin is in opposition to the Holy Spirit. He is not a distant force without discernment but is a present, perfect companion. God in us. This makes our bodies His home. "Don't you know that your body is a temple of the Holy Spirit who is in you?" the Bible asks. "You are not your own" (1 Cor. 6:19).

Any sinful choices we make, any moral compromises we allow, any evil entertainment we binge—it's not just us who's affected by it. The Holy Spirit is powerfully aware. He sees and feels it. The Scripture rightly warns us not to "grieve God's Holy Spirit" (Eph. 4:30), not to sadden and resist Him. He is not opposed to fun. He is opposed to you living without the love, joy, and peace that *He* gives and *sin* quenches.

So "let all bitterness, anger and wrath, shouting and slander be removed from you, along with all malice" (Eph. 4:31). "Flee sexual immorality" (1 Cor. 6:18). If you want to be satisfied by the Spirit, start by banishing any and all sins. They are competing with His loving presence inside you. Get them out of the way so you can start walking in freedom, joy, and peace with Him.

Be grateful and worshipful. Being *led* by the Spirit requires being *filled* with the Spirit and delighting in Him. And one of the biblical ways to walk in the Spirit is to embrace and enjoy an attitude of worship and gratitude. Believers are to be fountains of good conversations, having a readiness for praise and for God-honoring music, "speaking to one another in psalms, hymns, and spiritual songs, singing and making music with your heart to the Lord, giving thanks always for everything to God the Father in the name of our Lord Jesus Christ" (Eph. 5:19–20). When you present the Holy Spirit with a worshipful heart, a thankful heart—you give Him a heart ready for Him to bless and lead.

Be prayerful and in the Word. Prayer aligns our hearts and minds with the Spirit. He not only prompts prayer but guides and blesses our praying. Once when the believers in the early church had gathered and were praying, "the place where they were assembled was shaken, and they were all filled with the Holy Spirit and began to speak the word of God boldly" (Acts 4:31). Prayer says, *Come, Holy Spirit, come and fill me and reign in me*. So "pray at all times in the Spirit with every prayer and request" (Eph. 6:18), placing yourself completely at His disposal.

It's especially good to pray before and after you spend time in God's Word. He speaks in and through "the sword of the Spirit—which is the Word of God" (Eph. 6:17). The Spirit's guiding voice of direction is first heard plainly through the pages of Scripture as you prayerfully open it each day and let Him speak directly into your heart.

Be obedient to the Spirit's prompting. "If we live by the Spirit, let us also keep in step with the Spirit" (Gal. 5:25). As we are submitting, thanking, praising, and praying, God's Spirit will freely guide our thinking and decisions. He will prompt us with specific God-honoring ideas and desires, with practical ways for us to walk in love, serve Him, and help others.

You may not recognize His voice at first, but His promptings always align with the Word of God and are often confirmed by His peace and by the noticeable opening of doors for you to follow what He's directed you to do (Col. 3:15). Though our selfish and fearful flesh will tend to resist the promptings of the Spirit, we must be willing to take steps of faith to follow the Lord. He will give us favor, strength, and needed provision in His perfect timing. And He will be glorified by the results of our willing belief and surrender.

You can trust the Holy Spirit. He may prompt you to call or text an encouraging word to a specific friend at the perfect time. He may nudge you to pray for someone, share your faith with a stranger, serve a desperate need, write a song, or give a specific amount of money to a person. He may prompt you to turn away from something evil on a screen, to back out of an unhealthy relationship, or to leave a place where you might stumble into sin. Just follow His lead and watch what happens!

He loves you and will put you in the optimal position for maximum fruitfulness. So lean back on Jesus, stay connected to the vine, and let the one who knows everyone and everything lead you. "All who are led by the Spirit of God are sons of God" (Rom. 8:14 ESV).

Abide in Him, trust Him, and walk by faith. He will take care of the rest.

Dear Father, forgive me for anytime I have disobeyed or grieved Your Holy Spirit. Please fill me, lead me, and guide me to walk by Your Spirit and to more faithfully obey Your Word. Cleanse anything from my life that grieves You. Satisfy me with Your presence. Give me a willing heart to choose Your guidance over my own. Be glorified with my life in the days ahead! In Jesus' name. Amen.

Going Deeper

Psalm 143:10 • Micah 2:7 • Galatians 5:19–23

Part VIII

Victory

How Can I Overcome Evil?

32

OVERCOMING TEMPTATION

HOW SHOULD I RESPOND WHEN TEMPTED?

"You will know the truth, and the truth will set you free." John 8:32

Temptation is a fact of life, but we can now overcome it through our abiding relationship with Christ. No need to live defeated anymore by the things that held us captive in the past: the world, the flesh, the devil. Christ has overcome them all and He is alive in us (Col. 1:27).

Everyone is tempted by sin. Jesus was tempted. It's not a sign that you're failing. It's sometimes because you're a threat, like Jesus was a threat, and Satan is worried about you. But no matter how he tempts you to sin, he uses an old plan. He tries to convince you that you're all alone, that God has somehow failed you, that sin will satisfy you, and there's no escape from it. But those are all lies. Empty threats. God's Word says, "No temptation has come upon you except what is common to humanity. But God is faithful; he will not allow you to be tempted beyond what you are able, but with the temptation he will also provide the way out so that you may be able to bear it" (1 Cor. 10:13).

Sin is so unnecessary. We never need it to be happy in life, to love others, or to accomplish God's will. Jesus satisfies us *without* sin. The Holy Spirit never leaves us. The battle can feel ferocious, but there will always be a ready route to victory that we can freely take, if we'll only look for it.

Jesus has disarmed Satan through the power of the cross (Col. 2:15). So even at the height of temptation, when your enemy is demanding you give up and give in to him, realize he is waving an unloaded gun. You don't have to listen to him. You can call his bluff. To fear him is to have more faith in evil than in God, who is always faithful and will always provide what we need.

How do we respond when temptation comes knocking?

Be preemptive. We first prepare for success by finding our daily satisfaction in Christ. When we are daily receiving His Word and walking in the Father's love, our hunger for sin diminishes (1 John 2:15–17).

Second, we should look ahead to see where temptation is likely to come from. It's often obvious. "A prudent person sees evil and hides himself; but the naive proceed, and pay the penalty" (Prov. 27:12 NASB). Previous failures are some of our best indicators. Use them to your advantage. Being tempted periodically is common, but if you are daily tormented by temptation, there's usually a stronghold of the enemy in your heart from the past that you haven't dealt with. Defeated ground that's gone unreclaimed. Go back and repent of the *first time* you sinned in that area, and ask God to take back all of that ground from the enemy and be Lord over it in your life. "Submit to God. Resist the devil, and he will flee from you" (James 4:7).

Third, too many times we've left the same doors open to the tempter that he's used against us in the past. If we don't close off clear access points, we're almost inviting the devil to come back to us the same way with the same lies. Jesus warned, "If your eye causes you to stumble, pluck it out and throw it from you. It is better for you to enter life with one eye, than to have two eyes and be cast into the fiery hell" (Matt. 18:9 NASB). Vivid, but true. Take sin seriously. Preemptively prepare your life for victory instead of endless defeat.

The Lord ordered the children of Israel to "tear down," to "smash," to "cut down," to "burn" every false god that drew them away from Him (Deut. 7:5). And still today, we can be subject to modern-day versions of idols that can become "strongholds" in our lives (2 Cor. 10:4).

So it's a good idea to periodically go through your heart, your home, and your phone, and ask the Lord to identify anything that will give the enemy open access to repeatedly tempt you or attack your family. If the Lord clearly points something out to you, deal with it. Throw it out. Trust Him. It's part of growing in maturity and walking in victory. You likely won't miss it. Our instructions are to demolish them, to make *God* our stronghold, instead of enduring endless temptations (Ps. 27:1).

Stay in truth. The Bible says people who regularly walk in sin have "exchanged the truth of God for a lie" (Rom. 1:25). Like with Eve in the garden, the false arguments of temptation will initially sound as if they make sense, as if *this* sin is actually good for us and is just what we need. But God's truth exposes these lies. When we stay in the Word, reading it, hearing it, memorizing it, we will realize what's actually true, and it will set us free (John 8:31–32).

That's how Jesus battled intense temptation. With the Word. And it worked perfectly. He countered each of the enemy's arguments with truth, quoting Scriptures He had memorized (Matt. 4:1–11). He used specific verses that addressed specific temptations.

The Word of God is the sword of the Spirit. Use it to set yourself up for standing on truth instead of falling for the same old lies. "I have treasured your word in my heart," says the disciple of Christ, "so that I might not sin against you" (Ps. 119:11).

Keep abiding. The victory you're fighting so hard to achieve against temptation is actually "accomplished by God" (John 3:21). It's the fruit of staying attached to the vine.

That's what is so amazing about the devoted Christian life. Because of your faith in Christ, and because His death broke the power of sin over you, you are no longer "enslaved" to do what it says (Rom. 6:6). No matter what temptation says, sin is not your boss anymore. It is defeated and you are now dead to it. You are free to walk away, no longer dominated by it. And the Holy Spirit will give you the power to do it, the power you've been missing by trying to do it on your own.

Refuse to follow. Yes, say no. God's grace freely instructs us to "deny ungodliness and worldly desires" (Titus 2:12 NASB). We can freely tell the devil we're not available to sin anymore because we're too busy walking in victory over him. We can "take every thought captive to obey Christ" (2 Cor. 10:5). Victory is possible. Run to the Lord in prayer.

"Lord, I am not strong enough to withstand this temptation, but I know You are, and I know You are in me. Deliver me and satisfy me in You. Remind me I am Your beloved child and that You empower me now. Make this moment a trophy to Your grace. Be glorified in me."

Pray specifically, pray boldly, and pray confidently. Not just once, but whenever you need Him. He rescues you from an enemy who is already under His feet. "Blessed be the LORD, my rock who trains my hands for battle . . . my faithful love and my fortress, my stronghold and my deliverer. He is my shield, and I take refuge in him" (Ps. 144:1–2).

Father, how I praise You for meeting all my needs and never leaving me. You know my temptations and how I've failed You in the past. Thank You for the cross and that I no longer need to walk in defeat. I turn all my battles over to You today, asking You to lead me away from temptation and deliver me from all evil. Be victorious daily in me, through Christ. Amen.

Going Deeper

Proverbs 3:7–8 • Acts 19:17–20 • Hebrews 2:18

33

OVERCOMING THE ENEMY

HOW CAN I RESIST SATAN'S ATTACKS AGAINST ME?

Then Jesus told him, "Go away, Satan!
For it is written: Worship the Lord your God,
and serve only him." Matthew 4:10

You have a very real enemy. The devil (called Satan) and the demons that serve him all desire to attack everyone made in the image of God and anything that could bring God glory.

One of the reasons Jesus came to earth and shared our humanity was "that through his death he might destroy the one holding the power of death—that is, the devil—and free those who were held in slavery all their lives by the fear of death" (Heb. 2:14–15). Satan will be "cast out" because Jesus was "lifted up" (John 12:31–32).

He may seem like mythology to many, but not according to the Word of God. Fifteen books in the Bible talk about him. He's not merely a fictitious representation of evil. Jesus Himself was tempted by him (Matt. 4:1–10), called him "the father of lies" (John 8:44), trained His disciples against him (Luke 10:18–20), and boldly overcame him through the cross.

We do not have to fear the devil, but we should be fully aware of how he attacks and what to do when he does. Because, yes, he is real. He is active. He is crafty. He is persistent. He is insidious.

He is also defeated. So you are not defenseless. But it doesn't mean you can drop your guard.

We're not claiming the devil is behind every problem. He's not. Our own sinful flesh is also "opposed" to what God's Spirit desires (Gal. 5:17). This dark world, as we'll see in the next chapter, is resistant to the Word and the work of God in you and throughout the earth. But this axis of attack—the world, the flesh, and the devil—is behind so much pain and pressure each day. And Satan is the gang leader. This "ancient serpent, who is called the devil and Satan, the one who deceives the whole world . . . has come down to you with great fury, because he knows his time is short" (Rev. 12:9, 12).

He despises God, God's people, and God's glory with a vengeance. He's here only to "steal and kill and destroy" whatever he can, with whatever havoc he can create, with whatever short time he has left (John 10:10). But Jesus enables us to walk in victory and abundant life as overcomers in this world (1 John 5:4–5 NASB).

So buckle up and armor on. How should we biblically respond to Satan?

Stay aware. A call to arms against Satan is to "be sober-minded, be alert" (1 Pet. 5:8). He prowls readily, starts subtly, then ramps up attacks "in the evil day" when we're least prepared (Eph. 6:13). So disciples of Jesus must stay alert. "Let us not sleep, like the rest, but let us stay awake and be self-controlled" (1 Thess. 5:6). We're less likely to be surprised by the enemy if we're expecting him and if we know the playbook he's been using for centuries. He deceives, discourages, distracts, demeans, and divides.

Here's what happens if we don't. If we believe his accusations and we align our thinking and words with his arguments, they can form strongholds of bondage that daily torment us, causing us unnecessary fear, anger, doubt, and defeat. Strongholds are lies we believe that can prevent us from walking in victory. The devil and his demons mix facts and feelings with lies to see if we will agree with them. Satan cannot read our minds, but he is well aware of how susceptible we can be.

That's why we must "take every thought captive to obey Christ" (2 Cor. 10:5). Whenever an ungodly thought comes into your mind, ask yourself, "Is this pleasing to the Lord?" If not, cast it out, shut the door, and refuse to agree with it or dwell on it. It's like recognizing junk mail and deleting it.

Could Satan be the culprit behind a hateful, self-condemning thought that randomly flies into your head out of nowhere? Absolutely. He's the "father of lies," remember? Could he also be the sower of discord in your interpersonal relationships? He's known for planting bad seeds in good gardens (Matt. 13:38–39). Could he lead someone to gossip and blame you unfairly? Ask Joseph and Job. The name *Satan* means "accuser" or "adversary" (Rev. 12:10). Could he send perpetual distractions at pivotal times? Ask Nehemiah and Martha.

Satan has the spiritual gifts of discouragement and deception. He wants to derail your productivity and your peace. "God is not the author of confusion" (1 Cor. 14:33 NKJV), but Satan's demons can stir up bitter jealousy between siblings, coworkers, and church members that lead to "disorder and every evil thing" (James 3:15–16 NASB).

So before you overreact to a heated confrontation in a hazy situation, wake up and read the room. Do "not be taken advantage of by Satan. For we are not ignorant of his schemes" (2 Cor. 2:11).

Resist him. This is a key component of a winning battle plan. "Resist the devil, and he will flee from you" (James 4:7). Do not panic in fear or cower to his threats. Stand firm and push back in the name of Jesus. "Resist him, firm in the faith, knowing that the same kind of sufferings are being experienced by your fellow believers throughout the world" (1 Pet. 5:9).

This is spiritual warfare. Spiritual combat. "Our struggle is not against flesh and blood, but against the rulers, against the authorities, against the cosmic powers of this darkness, against evil, spiritual forces in the heavens" (Eph. 6:12).

Satan and his demons are never equal competitors with God. Christ's victory is already assured. That's why if you are abiding in Christ for your strength each day, no satanic force has the firepower to overcome you. You can use the powerful name of Jesus to resist him. Out loud, when necessary.

No, winning today doesn't stop him from attacking next month. He is an active adversary. But you will get stronger and wiser through every battle and victory. Scripture says to "put on the full armor of God so that you can stand against the schemes of the devil . . . so that you may be able to resist in the evil day" (Eph. 6:11, 13).

What are these pieces of armor? (1) "Truth like a belt around your waist." (2) "Righteousness like armor on your chest," like a breastplate. Sin weakens us, but staying right with God guards our hearts. (3) "Feet sandaled with readiness for the gospel of peace." (4) "The shield of faith with which you can extinguish all the flaming arrows of the evil one," all the lies and accusations that he shoots against us. (5) "The helmet of salvation." (6) "The sword of the Spirit—which is the word of God" (Eph. 6:14–17). Jesus rebuked Satan out loud with Scripture. We also can command Satan to leave because of the blood of Jesus and the power of His name.

Finally, we war through strategic prayer. We "pray at all times in the Spirit with every prayer and request, and stay alert with all perseverance and intercession for all the saints" (Eph. 6:18).

Then we're ready for battle. Ready to resist and then retake ground for the glory of God.

Father, I trust in Your might and power. Thank You for supplying me with everything needed for walking in truth, engaging evil, and being triumphant through the blood of Christ. Help me to close any access points and give no ground to the enemy. Make me strong in the Lord and in the power of His might. Deliver me from evil and temptation and grant me daily victory in You. I stand in Christ alone and in His name. Amen.

Going Deeper

Genesis 3:1–7 • Acts 13:8–10 • 1 John 5:18

34

Overcoming the World

How can I keep from being consumed by the culture?

"These things I have spoken to you so that in Me you may have peace. In the world you have tribulation, but take courage; I have overcome the world." John 16:33 NASB

Jesus loves the people of the world, but He does not trust the people of the world. It's what made so many of His religious critics angry with Him—because He wasn't above hanging out with "sinners" (Luke 15:2). But though He walked among and cared about all people, He didn't follow any of their backward or ungodly practices. He didn't buy into the empty priorities and opinions that characterize this culture. This world. This broken world.

This deceived world. This deceiving world.

Not the earth and the oceans. Not nature or the nations. Not *God's* world, the world He made. When the Bible speaks of "the world," think of it as the prevailing, sin-stained, self-serving culture of our day. Think of it as the cumulative depravity that is pulling you away toward its twisted beliefs, its evil practices, and its corrupted systems.

That's the "world" Jesus says He has now conquered for us so that we can have His peace even while continuing to live in a spiritual desert.

Our world consistently places great value on things that don't matter. As Jesus said, "What is highly admired by people is revolting in God's sight" (Luke 16:15). The world constantly champions pursuits that God calls foolishness, and it devalues what the Bible calls wisdom and worthy of embracing. We live in a polluted stream that is continually drifting away from the one true God and keeps relabeling "evil good and good evil" (Isa. 5:20). "What is worthless is exalted by the human race" (Ps. 12:8).

Yet it's still a point of tension, even for believers. The waves of the world's influence are continuously seducing and pushing you downstream into darker waters. The world dresses up depravity, making it promise you pleasure without mentioning the consequences. It advertises itself as a gateway to acceptance.

It looks and sounds convincing. Commercially polished. The abnormal is now the new normal. Yet it harbors and hides the backlash of death. It is constantly driving you away from "the good, pleasing, and perfect will of God" (Rom. 12:2), along with lots of other people who "are surprised that you don't join them in the same flood of wild living" (1 Pet. 4:4).

But though we must live in this world, like Jesus lived in this world, loving the people of this world, we must choose not to be enslaved by the lies and allurements of this world.

We live in the light. Jesus came "as light into the world, so that everyone who believes in me would not remain in darkness" (John 12:46). Before we believed in Him, "we walked according to the ways of this world" (Eph. 2:2), having no desire to resist it, rebuke it, or even to realize it. Satan has quietly "blinded the minds of the unbelievers to keep them from seeing the light of the gospel of the glory of Christ" (2 Cor. 4:4). That was us at one time, ignorantly living in the dark.

Until Jesus. The grace of God appeared, "instructing us to deny godlessness and worldly lusts and to live in a sensible, righteous, and godly way" (Titus 2:12), so that we now "walk in the light as he himself is in the light" (1 John 1:7). That's good for us.

But it can be dangerous too.

We live hated by the darkness. Just as it hated Jesus. "If you were of the world," He said, "the world would love you as its own. However, because you are not of the world, but I have chosen you out of it, the world hates you" (John 15:19).

Do not be surprised by this. Ask Daniel's friends Shadrach, Meshach, and Abednego how accepted they felt after they quietly declined from worshiping the king's golden idol (Dan. 3). Ask Paul how things went after he upset the metalworkers in Ephesus by saying the silver statues they manufactured were false gods (Acts 19:23–28). When we merely live in the light of integrity and morality within the culture, our lives can expose the evil that is so prevalent in the darkness. It's what makes us unpopular. Targets. But by the power of Christ, it's what makes us free. Liberated from the lies. Overcomers.

We live transformed. This is the peaceful space reserved for those who are devoted to Jesus. Risk-free? Maybe not. Pain-free? Certainly not. "In fact, all who want to live a godly life in Christ Jesus will be persecuted" (2 Tim. 3:12). But the prize of living within God's will is a life that matters in eternity and a joy that keeps on giving. We are in the world, but not of the world.

"Do not be conformed to this age," Paul said, "but be transformed by the renewing of your mind" (Rom. 12:2). Be constantly *renewed*. That's the key. Stay plugged in to what is true and eternal. Feed on the Word. Let it fill your thoughts, update your perspectives, and challenge the easy status quo.

It's what resets your old presets. Instead of going back to the same old polluted wells that have fed you so much vanity and stupidity before, your renewed mind helps you see they've been wasting your time. Draining you dry. They lie. Over time, you see that what the world prizes and promises is usually the opposite of what you should pursue. What they are selling, you don't need. And what they are mocking and attacking is often what's worthy of your respect.

If the world demands that you hit the gas and swerve left, expect God's plan most likely to involve slowing down and exiting off to the right. Walk in humility and lovingkindness toward all people, of course, but don't allow the world to force you into its mold. Surrendered disciples who become more and more like Jesus discover their conquering skills from Him by actively cultivating a renewed mind.

The culture says to follow your heart; the Bible says to lead your heart and renew your mind. The more you trust and follow Jesus, the less you will end up following the world. But you will live as an overcomer in Christ and never regret taking the road less traveled.

"Do not love the world or the things in the world. If anyone loves the world, the love of the Father is not in him. For everything in the world—the lust of the flesh, the lust of the eyes, and the pride in one's possessions—is not from the Father, but is from the world. And the world with its lust is passing away, but the one who does the will of God remains forever" (1 John 2:15–17).

Father, renew my mind in Christ. Saturate me in truth. Show me the path to travel so that I can walk in freedom and victory in this world. Set me free from the lies of the culture and grow in me a life of surrender. Send me to those in the world You want to serve and help set free. Make my light shine with the brightness of Your glory. In Jesus' name. Amen.

Going Deeper

John 3:19–21 • 1 Corinthians 1:20–25 • Colossians 2:8–10

35

Overcoming Sin

How can I repent of the sin in my life?

"There is joy in the presence of God's angels over one sinner who repents." Luke 15:10

Sin is a Judas. It greets us with a smile, kisses us like a friend, then betrays us like an enemy. Sin is a spiritual cancer. It puts down roots, grows, spreads, and contaminates, hurting us as the sinner as well as those we sin against.

Even after we've given our lives to Christ, we remain in a battle against it. Even after we've been forgiven from the *penalty* of our sin, even after we've been set free from the ongoing *power* of our sin, any of us can commit almost any sin if we stop abiding with Christ and we underestimate the enemy. "For we all stumble in many ways" (James 3:2).

There are many examples of this in Scripture. Even Adam in all his innocence, even Noah after the flood, even David after all his worship and his victories for God, even Solomon with all his wisdom, even Peter with all his devotion—each of them had his moments when he took his eyes off the Lord, when he drifted out of fellowship with Him. "Whoever thinks he stands must be careful not to fall" (1 Cor. 10:12).

But how do we respond when we're the one who fails to keep our guard up against the enemy? When we're like Adam after eating the fruit? Like David after his adultery? Like Peter after he denied Jesus? What should we do when, even with all the resources we've been given in Christ, we continue to struggle with one or more areas of defeat?

Follow the voice of the Holy Spirit. Satan will say you've gone too far, that you cannot be redeemed or used by God again, that the Lord has rejected you, that you have no hope. These things are actually true of *him*, but not of you. The Holy Spirit is the one whose voice you can trust. Listen to Him. Listen to His Word. He lovingly convicts you to turn back and be restored.

Remember your identity in the Lord. If Jesus is your Lord, He's already forgiven you of all your past, present, and future sins. "He erased the certificate of debt, with its obligations, that was against us and opposed to us, and has taken it away by nailing it to the cross" (Col. 2:14). You are no longer under sin's condemnation. You are no longer a slave of sin. You are God's beloved child, set free from sin through Jesus. You were once guilty and condemned, "but you were washed, you were sanctified, you were justified in the name of the Lord Jesus Christ and by the Spirit of our God" (1 Cor. 6:11). Always remember that!

Run to your heavenly Father. Jesus expressed how God responds to a repentant sinner in His story of the prodigal son (Luke 15:11–32). This young man had squandered his inheritance. He'd feasted on his own lusts. He'd walked in wickedness until finally cratering in defeat. But when his father saw his repentant son coming home, he "was filled with compassion. He ran, threw his arms around his neck, and kissed him" (Luke 15:20). His beloved child had come home! The father's grace was so much greater than the son's sin. All his father wanted to do was "celebrate" (v. 23).

That's your Father's heart toward you. He is eager for you to come back to Him. That's why, in those moments when you've allowed your flesh to fall again, there's no need for a long gap between the moment you *realize* what you've done and you *repent* over what you've done. It can be almost instantaneous. Running back to your Father's side again. Ready to abide again.

The Bible repeatedly describes our Father as "a forgiving God, gracious and compassionate, slow to anger and abounding in faithful love" (Neh. 9:17). He has poured out all the holy wrath your sin deserves on His precious Son Jesus, so that no more of it is coming your way. That's how much He loves you. Let sin deceive you no longer.

Fully confess it. The truth sets you free. "The one who conceals his sins will not prosper, but whoever confesses and renounces them will find mercy" (Prov. 28:13).

Confession is where truth crashes into the darkness and exposes the deception that sin depends on for its oxygen. As David said, "When I kept silent, my bones became brittle from my groaning all day long. For day and night your hand was heavy on me; my strength was drained as in the summer's heat." Then what? "Then I acknowledged my sin to you and did not conceal my iniquity. I said, 'I will confess my transgressions to the LORD,' and you forgave the guilt of my sin" (Ps. 32:3–5).

Forgiveness and fellowship readily await us: "If we confess our sins, he is faithful and righteous to forgive us our sins and to cleanse us from all unrighteousness" (1 John 1:9).

Repent of it. Repentance means to turn around. To make a U-turn. Not just to clean ourselves up but to head in the other direction. By the grace of our God and the strength of our Savior, we change course. We've seen enough. We're turning this ship around. We're doing things differently from here on.

That's what David did after his sin with Bathsheba. An unrepentant person would never have come back from that kind of horrific fall. But he *confessed* it openly to God: "Against you—you alone—I have sinned and done this evil in your sight" (Ps. 51:4). He *repented*: "Create a clean heart for me and renew a steadfast spirit within me" (v. 10). Then he *turned* to discipling others: "I will teach the rebellious your ways, and sinners will return to you" (v. 13).

Start walking in truth again. That's what disciples do. They go find one or more close friends who can pray for them, who can help them walk back into the light. Left to ourselves, we'll keep deceiving ourselves. But "confess your sins to one another and pray for one another, so that you may be healed" (James 5:16). The Lord has provided grace and complete cleansing through the cross. He is faithful to forgive. Sometimes it takes a team working together, being honest with one another, to get the light just right for getting our sin pointed out.

As we talk about overcoming sin, we want to continually come back to the core aspects of our relationship with God: *abiding* in Him and walking *daily* with Him. Abiding is not only the secret to bearing fruit but also to overcoming strongholds.

Not to-do lists, check marks, or religious rules. These may have some value, but God alone can set us free from the bondage of sin. We don't do it by wallowing in self-pity or trying to amp up our self-discipline. Only by God's grace and power can we overcome the ungodly things in our lives that previously held us captive in defeat. Knowing our compassionate Father, surrendering to Jesus as Lord, and following the leadership of the Holy Spirit enable us to walk in a new victory like never before.

"How joyful is the one whose transgression is forgiven, whose sin is covered! How joyful is a person whom the LORD does not charge with iniquity and in whose spirit is no deceit!" (Ps. 32:1–2).

Father, I confess my sins to You and ask for Your mercy and forgiveness. Thank You for loving me more than I've loved my sin. I repent of it. I turn from it. Wash me clean and change my heart. Strengthen me, Lord, to walk this path away from where I've been, home to where I belong, always abiding and living in Your presence and loving arms. In the name of Jesus. Amen.

Going Deeper

Psalm 32:9–10 • Daniel 9:15–19 • 2 Corinthians 7:9–11

36

Being an Overcomer

How do I deal with difficult times?

In him was life, and that life was the light of men. That light shines in the darkness, and yet the darkness did not overcome it. John 1:4–5

Life can be extremely hard. Scripture does not hold back from acknowledging the pain and suffering people can experience on earth. Though heaven is our home, we still presently live in a dark and broken world. We should expect tribulation but not be afraid of it (1 Pet. 4:12). Even the godliest people will endure seasons of great sickness, tragic loss, bitter rejection, false accusation, or unfair persecution (2 Tim. 3:12). The question is not whether we will suffer in this short life, but how will we intentionally glorify God through the midst of the fire?

Sometimes God is most glorified by performing a miracle. Answering prayers. Doing the impossible. Rescuing

His children out of terrible situations. He did it throughout Scripture and still does it today around the world. This is our hope, our prayer—our first choice!

But at other times, God is most glorified by powerfully enabling His children to walk through suffering with unbelievable strength, resilient faith, and surpassing joy, all while He's helping us model the character of Christ and the hope of the gospel to a watching world. The apostle Paul demonstrated this reality. He stood as ready for death as for deliverance. His chief hope was that "Christ will be highly honored in my body, whether by life or by death. For me, to live is Christ and to die is gain" (Phil. 1:20–21).

No one, though, overcame like Jesus. He never feared difficulties. He constantly prevailed over hard circumstances, even redeeming them, turning them all into powerful ministry opportunities that only advanced His kingdom.

When Jesus was tempted by the devil, He counterattacked with Scripture. When He was rejected in His hometown, He launched out and expanded His ministry. When He was falsely accused by the Pharisees, He leveraged it to teach truth while confronting their hypocrisy. No criticism could discourage him. No circumstance could stop Him. Every satanic attack only backfired. He turned it around for His own advantage. When demons railed at Him, Jesus rebuked them. When Peter denied Him, Jesus still restored him. When His disciples panicked under pressure, He confronted their fear and grew their faith.

Jesus is the greatest overcomer of all time. When hated, He loved. When cursed, He blessed. When nailed to a cross, He forgave and saved. When buried, He rose! Regardless of the occasion, Jesus used everything at all times as an opportunity to fulfill His mission, to model His love, and to glorify His heavenly Father (John 17:4).

But not only did He embody victory Himself. He calls each of us who follow Him to adopt this same faith-fueled mentality as well. He said when people "insult you and persecute you and falsely say every kind of evil against you because of me," you should "be glad and rejoice, because your reward is great in heaven" (Matt. 5:11–12).

He said to "love your enemies and pray for those who persecute you" (Matt. 5:44). When we are wronged, He taught us to forgive—"seventy times seven" (Matt. 18:22). And when we're the one who's wronged someone else, He said to "go and be reconciled" (Matt. 5:24). He told us never to lose heart but to walk by faith, to ramp up our praying instead of giving up (Luke 18:1).

Consider Paul again, who was in the very center of God's will when he was abandoned, stoned, and shipwrecked during his ministry (2 Cor. 11:22–27). Instead of getting depressed, he rejoiced after realizing God was powerfully using his hardships to keep him humble while rapidly advancing the gospel (Phil. 1:12). He said, "Therefore, I will most gladly boast all the more about my weaknesses, so that Christ's power may reside in me. So I take pleasure in weaknesses, insults, hardships, persecutions, and in difficulties, for the sake of Christ. For when I am weak, then I am strong" (2 Cor. 12:9–10).

In Acts 16, Paul and Silas were beaten and imprisoned for proclaiming the gospel. Did they forsake their faith or accept failure? Not in the least. At midnight they were "praying and singing hymns to God" where the other inmates could hear (v. 25). God stepped in and helped them unexpectedly win the chief jailer and his entire household to Christ. An amazing comeback!

We, too, are representing the King of kings and the Lord of lords in our generation. As His body, His bride, and His disciples, we are all commanded not to be "overcome by evil," but to "overcome evil with good" (Rom. 12:21 NASB). For God's divine power has given us everything we need for glorifying Him in any situation (2 Pet. 1:3).

When we know Christ, we become overcomers through Him. For the one who overcame sin, death, and the grave is living inside of us. When the world panics, we can still walk in His peace with our hearts full of hope. We know Jesus is always with us in every season, shepherding us throughout every valley. In the worst crises, we can lift our eyes and still rejoice, knowing our God is sovereign (Ps. 103:19), that our intimacy with Christ is only deepening through harder times. Scripture says our endurance, character, and hope will only become stronger each day as we trust Him during tribulation (Rom. 5:1–5). It's in the darkest hours that believers truly shine the brightest.

So, yes, expect very challenging times to come. But at the same time, remember God's bigger picture. Life is a vapor, and eternity is forever. Until heaven, we have His Word to teach us, His Spirit to empower us, and His promises to carry us.

"Who can separate us from the love of Christ? Can affliction or distress or persecution or famine or nakedness or danger or sword? . . . No, in all these things we are more than conquerors through him who loved us" (Rom. 8:35, 37). Regardless of what happens, nothing "will be able to separate us from the love of God that is in Christ Jesus our Lord" (v. 39).

What if you knew in every trial or hardship, God was going to work everything out for His glory and your good? Because that is exactly what He plans to do. Do not worry or fear. He loves you and is always with you (Matt. 28:20). You can trust Him either to rescue you from the battle or to walk with you through the fire. Either way, you can walk in perpetual victory by rejoicing always, praying without ceasing, and in everything giving thanks (1 Thess. 5:16–18)!

Heavenly Father, I praise You for being powerful and present in hard circumstances. You've provided everything I need in Christ and will never leave me. Thank You for bearing my burdens and carrying me through the toughest battles. Deliver me, strengthen me, grow me, comfort me, and be glorified mightily through me, O God. In Jesus' name. Amen.

Going Deeper

Romans 8:31–39 • 1 Corinthians 15:58 • 1 Peter 4:1–2

PART IX

LIFESTYLE

How Can I Daily Live Out My Faith?

37

LIVING A LIFE OF HUMILITY

HOW CAN I EMPTY MY HEART OF PRIDE?

"Everyone who exalts himself will be humbled, and the one who humbles himself will be exalted." Luke 14:11

Humility is at the heart of true discipleship because it is the heart of who Jesus is.

He humbled Himself more than anyone who's ever existed. He was the eternal God who stepped out of heaven, down into human flesh. On earth, He still had every right and reason for being center stage at all times. Imagine what it required of Him not to judge everyone in comparison to Himself, not to always feel and act superior to them. Always the smartest person in the room. Yet He could say, without the slightest bit of deception, "I am lowly and humble in heart" (Matt. 11:29). He made the ongoing and deliberate decision to continually keep humbling Himself, just as we can make the same decision.

We must humble ourselves to be like Jesus.

"God opposes the proud but gives grace to the humble" (James 4:6 ESV). It's one of the main themes of Scripture, the universal contrast between pride and humility. God looks past those who are haughty and arrogant and full of themselves. The self-made. The self-exalting. He intentionally chooses the underdog. He prefers the meek and humble. He draws to Himself those who are "insignificant and despised in the world," those who are "viewed as nothing—to bring to nothing what is viewed as something, so that no one may boast in his presence" (1 Cor. 1:28–29).

Because once anyone knows the truth about God, and the truth about themselves, there's honestly no justifiable boasting in His presence.

Ask Nebuchadnezzar, who was bragging one moment about the great kingdom he'd built "by my vast power and for my majestic glory" (Dan. 4:30). The next moment he was crawling in insanity, roaming the countryside like an animal. Ask Herod, basking in the praise of the crowd for having "the voice of a god and not of a man" (Acts 12:22). Before he knew what hit him, he was struck dead for not giving glory to God Himself.

Anytime in Scripture when someone encountered the reality of God's glory, that person was very quickly humbled. Any nose up in the air became a face in the dirt.

Job was already a righteous man with integrity and wisdom, but when confronted by the power of God's awesome voice from a whirlwind, Job responded, "I reject my words and am sorry for them; I am dust and ashes" (Job 42:6). The prophet Isaiah, seeing a vision of the Lord exalted on His throne, suddenly cried out, "Woe is me for I am ruined because I am a man of unclean lips" (Isa. 6:5). John the apostle, the disciple that Jesus loved (John 19:26), was faced with a glorious vision of the resurrected Christ and immediately "fell at his feet like a dead man" (Rev. 1:17).

God's presence overwhelmed each of these people. You could tell by what they said. Or didn't say. They were terrified in awestruck wonder.

The closer we get to the Lord, the more humble we become. And if we don't humble ourselves, God promises to help humble us, because "if anyone considers himself to be something when he is nothing, he deceives himself" (Gal. 6:3). Arrogance is disgusting to watch, but it deceptively justifies itself in our own blinded hearts. Why do we so hate to see pride in others, yet we so willingly tolerate it in ourselves? So much pride.

So let's do something about it. Whenever we've let self-deception rise up, take over, and take the credit, we must come into the light and get honest before God, remembering that no one will boast at the judgment in His presence. We must kneel before His awesomeness, realizing "it is He who has made us, and not we ourselves" (Ps. 100:3 NASB), that "all things are through him, and we exist through him" (1 Cor. 8:6).

Just as you "don't boast about yourself before the king" (Prov. 25:6), you humble yourself in the presence of the King of kings. Where pride entices us to want to shine above others, humility understands God shines above us all. Pride is the lie we keep telling ourselves, but humility is the bravery to face the truth. And the truth, as we've said so often, sets us free (John 8:32).

"Where, then, is boasting? It is excluded" (Rom. 3:27). We've been given new life in Christ completely by the work He did, not by anything we did. As Paul said, "What do you have that you didn't receive?" (1 Cor. 4:7). Nothing. Everything's been given, nothing earned. So "the wise person should not boast in his wisdom; the strong should not boast in his strength; the wealthy should not boast in his wealth. But the one who boasts should boast in this: that he understands and knows me—that I am the LORD" (Jer. 9:23–24). He always has the final word.

Pride is at the root of so much sin. Fueling countless problems. Causing endless stress. Giving people false permission to do things God clearly forbids. It poisons thinking. Corrupts relationships. It's the underlying source of so much anger and greed, lust and immorality. It is the fire behind all our jealousy. Unforgiveness is rooted in pride. Ingratitude. Even many insecurities and anxieties. Wars are started over pride. Churches split over pride. Marriages fall apart because of pride. Friendships die by pride. God, help us to humble ourselves!

We need humility. Christ's humility. It brings the opposite of these horrors. It heals and helps. It helps us repent. God has grace ready for us to help draw us to humility. To truth and purity. To freedom and peace.

Moses surely knew this grace. Though he was the great deliverer of the people of Israel, he was "a very humble man, more so than anyone on the face of the earth" (Num. 12:3). He'd seen the burning bush, the plagues of Egypt, the parting of the Red Sea, God's glory on the mountain. Moses knew he was nothing compared to God.

John the Baptist also found this grace. Though the large audiences he attracted through his ministry began to dwindle once Jesus arrived, John gladly said, "He must increase, but

I must decrease" (John 3:30). He knew humility was the right response in every circumstance.

But our greatest example remains Jesus Himself, "who, existing in the form of God, did not consider equality with God as something to be exploited. Instead he emptied himself by assuming the form of a servant, taking on the likeness of humanity" (Phil. 2:6–7).

This is the way. Walk in it.

The door to salvation is a low door. We must humble ourselves to get through it. The door that leads us to effectiveness as a follower of Christ is low as well—the beautiful door of humility. Through it, we can bow in prayer, in repentance, in worship, in adoration, and in service to wash the feet of others. But it is also God's chosen requirement for raising us up and blessing us with His abundant fruit as a disciple.

Being humbled will happen to everyone soon enough. Just wait. Blessed are those who humble themselves now. First and often. For God will exalt them.

Heavenly Father, You reign in majesty. You are owner of all and deserve all the glory. Open my eyes to Your majesty and clothe me with humility. May I receive Your grace and esteem others as better than myself. Make me like Jesus. Use me as Your humble servant. In Jesus' name. Amen.

Going Deeper

Daniel 4:37 • Philippians 2:3–4 • James 4:6–10

38

Living a Life of Reconciliation

Who needs to hear me apologize?

"If you are offering your gift on the altar, and there you remember that your brother or sister has something against you, leave your gift there in front of the altar. First go and be reconciled with your brother or sister." Matthew 5:23–24

Following Christ is a relational experience. Not religious rules. Not trying harder. Not chasing a standard for showing off. It's being in relationship with the Father, through the Son, by the Spirit. The relationship shared among the three persons of the Trinity is indicative of the relationship that God has invited us into. In Christ.

So when you're deliberately abiding in Him, when you're seeking to stay close and clean in your relationship with Him, He will often bring to mind someone you're not in a right relationship with. Someone who honestly "has something against you."

Someone you need to reconcile with.

God knows the collateral damage the devil can manufacture from any kind of brokenness in a relationship. Especially in your family, your marriage, but really anywhere—at church, at work, with anyone. God wants every heart free, open, and made right with the people living around them. He wants every chain broken that could possibly be holding you back from being completely ready and available to Him. He wants nothing dragging you down or creating an obstruction to hearing His voice or following without reservation.

In fact, to anyone who thinks what God wants most from them is more religious service, Jesus made it clear: "If you are offering your gift at the altar" and God brings an offended person to mind, "leave your gift there in front of the altar" and go do your best to make it right. Get up and leave church if needed. Pause your worship. Get out of your prayer closet and get into your car. Your worship and your quiet time can wait. "If possible, as far as it depends on you, live at peace with everyone" (Rom. 12:18). And today, in this moment, He means *that* person. The one you're thinking about right now. Yes, it's time.

The context for this teaching is Jesus' Sermon on the Mount, specifically where He was challenging people's tolerance of their own anger. He said a person might pridefully feel as though they'd kept the sixth commandment—"Thou shalt not kill" (Exod. 20:13 KJV)—as long as they hadn't actually murdered someone. But, no, being angry at someone is the same exact offense, just hidden in the heart. Anger doesn't only *lead* to murder, it makes you *punishable* for murder in the eyes of God.

And that's a problem demanding immediate attention.

So if you've had words with someone or done things to hurt someone, go apologize and ask forgiveness. If you've stolen something, go pay it back. If you've not kept a promise you made, go take care of it today or reinforce your intention to start working on it right away. If you've injured or spoken ill of someone's character, go make it right. Admit what you've done, seek forgiveness, and help them to heal. Even if you sincerely believe this other person shoulders most of the blame for whatever's caused your relationship to turn sour, Jesus said to be the first to own up to your part of it. Even if you've done nothing wrong but they are struggling with bitterness in their heart against you, Jesus wants you to go help them work things out.

Make it a priority. First thing. "Go and be reconciled with your brother or sister."

There's speed involved. There's humility involved. Maybe cost and inconvenience involved. But there are much bigger stakes involved. Anytime any of us backs away from dealing openly and honestly with our sin, we suffer a noticeable lack of peace, joy, and power in our spiritual life. Our fellowship with the Lord feels forced and dry. Something is holding us back. We're not being ourselves, the new person He's made us to be.

And in ways we may not see, we're even contributing to the ineffectiveness of the church, across the body of Christ. Because if "my people, who bear my name, humble themselves, pray and seek my face, and turn from their evil ways," the Lord says, "then I will hear from heaven, forgive their sin, and heal their land" (2 Chron. 7:14). Revival will wait on restored relationships. Starting with yours. You can be God's spark.

Even believers who hold strong stances on political and moral issues of the day can easily ignore their own hidden bitterness and anger. Satan loves and uses this division. But who knows what outpourings of repentance and grace are hanging right above our heads, ready to spread like wildfire through our churches, our communities, our nation? If only God's people would get serious about being reconciled with others. Being kind and tenderhearted. Apologetic. Genuinely humble. Showing mercy. Proving to be peacemakers.

"Therefore, as God's chosen ones, holy and dearly loved, put on compassion, kindness, humility, gentleness, and patience, bearing with one another and forgiving one another if anyone has a grievance against another. Just as the Lord has forgiven you, so you are also to forgive. Above all, put on love, which is the perfect bond of unity" (Col. 3:12–14).

Here's the question: Is there anyone in your life right now who could point his or her finger at you and say, "You wronged me and you've never made it right"? A parent? A child? A spouse? Anyone? If you don't know, but suspect it, then go and ask. Just in case.

Help them to heal. Go and be reconciled.

Father, show me anyone I need to go reconcile with. Show me what I've done and need to do. Make me a peacemaker and catalyst for healing and revival, Your ambassador for reconciliation. Show Your mercy through me. Reunite what's broken. Give me the joy of renewed relationship with others as a sign of Your goodness, as an opening for You to do even greater things through me. I pray through Christ. Amen.

Going Deeper

Genesis 33:8–11 • 2 Corinthians 5:18–19 • 1 Timothy 2:8

39

LIVING A LIFE OF FAITH

WHAT DIFFERENCE DOES FAITH MAKE?

Jesus said to him, "'If you can'? Everything is possible for the one who believes." Immediately the father of the boy cried out, "I do believe; help my unbelief!" Mark 9:23–24

When you think about what separates the true disciple of Jesus from everyone else, it's not just faith. It's *living* by faith. Everything believers think or do should be influenced by their faith in Christ. We're saved by faith, we grow in faith, we pray in faith, and we obey in faith.

But what is faith? It's a word so frequently used, not only in church and religious circles but throughout common culture, that we owe it to ourselves to be clear on what the Bible means when God talks about faith.

"Faith is the assurance of things hoped for, the conviction of things not seen" (Heb. 11:1 ESV). Being sure of something unseen. Biblical faith in the one living God is the residing confidence that everything He says is true, that everything He's promised He will do. It's being sure enough in His character that we are compelled to act on what He says and also to expect a response from Him. He invites our faith. "Without faith it is impossible to please God, since the one who draws near to him must believe that he exists and that he rewards those who seek him" (Heb. 11:6).

It's not the same as *blind* faith. Believers in Jesus live for a God who has proven Himself credible and trustworthy—the God of creation, of the Scriptures, of Israel, of fulfilled prophecy, transformed lives, renewed minds, and answered prayer. People may *doubt* God. By continuing to question Him, they may *deny* God, being not only uncertain of Him but intentionally rejecting Him. Yet they can't *disprove* God. No one can. You can't disprove truth. Because everything about truth, and the God of truth, aligns with reality. "Let God be true, even though everyone is a liar" (Rom. 3:4). The honest seeker cannot escape the fact that life consistently aligns with what the Word of God says.

Yet we should never expect God to answer every question we can contrive or explain every detail of the future before we finally choose to trust and obey Him. That's why it's called faith. And faith is what we need. It's part of this relationship He's designed to have with us. He can be counted on. He already knows it. All we really need to know to take the next step is that He can be counted on. That's faith.

Faith works. It is living and active. "We walk by faith," the Bible says, "not by sight" (2 Cor. 5:7). It's true we don't do anything to earn our salvation. But if that faith of ours is real, it will shift us into motion. "Faith, if it does not have works, is dead by itself" (James 2:17).

Walking by faith takes work. It's an effort. It involves a lot of *asking* by faith, *seeking* by faith, *knocking* by faith (Matt. 7:7–8). Think of it as a continual cycle, like a running faith engine, firing on all cylinders.

God told Joshua to lead the people of Israel into the Promised Land, but then Joshua had to go do it—keep praying, keep gathering intel, keep adjusting himself to what God told him to do. He wasn't following a detailed plan; he was seeking and following the God who knew *every* detail and was guiding each step. The job of faith is to get us climbing into the yoke with Jesus, walking in step with Him, seeking His face, and relying on Him to strengthen us and provide for us through everything we do. "Show me your faith without works, and I will show you faith by my works" (James 2:18). "Everything that is not from faith is sin" (Rom. 14:23).

Faith expects. We know that God consistently rewards faith. It's up to Him *how* He does it. We just need to know and trust that He *will* do it. This single shift in perspective—expecting God to reward faith—changes how you approach any situation. You can always know that something good is going to happen if God is in it. You can bank on it. Even bad news and evil events should come into the ears of believers through a filter of faith. We already know that our God is always going to bring good out of anything that happens (Rom. 8:28–29).

Every person whose name appears in Hebrews 11—the "Hall of Faith"—was greatly blessed by God for trusting Him. Whenever you read this chapter, ask yourself: (1) What did God say to them? (2) What did they do by faith? (3) What did they gain, receive, or obtain as a reward? (4) How was God glorified?

Abel received God's approval (Heb. 11:4). Enoch was spared death (v. 5). Noah was saved from the flood (v. 7). Sarah was given the ability to conceive a child (v. 11). Abraham received that child back to life (v. 19). And it keeps on going. People "conquered kingdoms, administered justice, obtained promises, shut the mouths of lions" (v. 33). Others "escaped the edge of the sword, gained strength in weakness, became mighty in battle, and put foreign armies to flight" (v. 34). Even those who were tortured and lost their lives, refusing to renounce Him, were given grace and miraculous strength in their suffering and were assured of gaining "a better resurrection" (v. 35). Faith works because faith expects God to work.

Faith grows. Jesus said to the father of a demon-possessed boy, "Everything is possible for the one who believes" (Mark 9:23). What did the man do? He asked for more faith.

That's how it grows. We ask Him for it. We read His Word and believe His Word when we read it. When hard times come, we trust God and endure. Don't be shocked if He takes you to the last hour, where it seems He's failed, where you're tempted to give in and give up. But that's where faith takes deep root and quickly grows. That's where faith gets so much stronger, when He powerfully does what only God can do, and we add it to our prayer "walls of remembrance" that remind us He is faithful and that we should never doubt Him again.

Do you want to grow in faith? Then stop praying only general prayers, only "bless me" and "bless Mom" and "bless everybody in the whole world" prayers. Pray specific prayers. Big prayers. Write them down. Put His Word to the test. Dare to go where only a strong follower of a faithful God would go.

And while you're going—while your faith is at work and expecting—take note and recognize what He does.

Whenever He tells you by His Word and His Spirit to do something—whatever it is—step forward with the light He's given you, and He will light up the next leg of your journey. How do we know? Because we've seen Him do it. Time after time. Year after year. That's not what faith is just supposed to say. It's what faith does. It's what faith knows.

You can trust Him. He is about to grow your faith.

Father, I see what You have made and I hear what You have done. I do believe. Help my unbelief. Build me into a person of great faith. Show me what prayers I need to pray and what steps I need to take. Help me to trust You more and more each day. I ask by faith in Jesus. Amen.

Going Deeper

Psalm 27:13 • 2 Corinthians 1:8–11 • Philippians 4:6–7

40

Living a Life of Submission

Do I have any other authority than Jesus?

"You would have no authority over me at all," Jesus answered him, "if it hadn't been given you from above." John 19:11

People have a natural tendency to resist and rebel against authority. It comes as a standard feature on all humanity. Kids, teens, and adults all want to be free to do what they want, and authority can stand in the way of that. Thankfully! Jesus was countercultural in that He consistently respected authority when He lived on the earth. He even continues to respect the Father's authority now. The Bible reveals that God intentionally establishes and uses human authorities to carry out His purposes in ways the world does not realize or understand.

Jesus fully understood the power and importance of authority. He submitted to the authority of His parents (Luke 2:51). He even recognized the authority of Caesar (Mark 12:17). He honored the faith of a Roman centurion who understood that Jesus had the authority to heal (Matt. 8:5–10). Most remarkably, Jesus submitted to the authority of Pontius Pilate, who presided over the trial that led to Christ's execution.

Pilate was an unbelieving pagan, and his decision to scourge and crucify Jesus seemed so unjust. But God's plan was not thwarted by Pilate's sinfulness. God was intentionally using Pilate's authority to bring about ultimate justice through Christ.

In His exchange with this Roman governor, Jesus provided an insight into authority that should shape the way we view and respond to it today. Recall the scene. Jesus, despite being the Son of God, let them drag Him before a human court on false charges of blasphemy. Why? Because in the garden of Gethsemane, He had already submitted His will to the authority of His Father. And now in an astonishing demonstration of restraint, He refused to defend Himself when questioned.

Pilate was perplexed. "Don't you know that I have the authority to release you and the authority to crucify you?" (John 19:10). Listen closely to Jesus' answer: "You would have no authority over me at all," He said, "if it hadn't been given you from above" (v. 11). Jesus knew that all authority ultimately derives from a single source: God.

"For everything was created by him, in heaven and on earth, the visible and the invisible, whether thrones or dominions or rulers or *authorities*—all things have been created through him and for him" (Col. 1:16, emphasis added). It can mean only one thing: *our obedience to authorities is part of God's plan to carry out His purposes for our lives.*

Let's consider the human authorities God has placed on earth. None of them are perfect. But what does His Word say about how we should relate to each of them?

Government. "Let everyone submit to the governing authorities, since there is no authority except from God, and the authorities that exist are instituted by God. So then, the one who resists the authority is opposing God's command" (Rom. 13:1–2). Why? "For it is God's servant" that He has placed over you "for your good" (v. 4), for your protection, for the keeping of order. All human authorities are sinful, broken, ignorant, and imperfect. But God can and will use them.

Family. "Wives, submit to your husbands as to the Lord" (Eph. 5:22), even as husbands submit to the authority of Jesus in helping them sacrificially love their wives "just as Christ loved the church and gave himself for her" (v. 25). Children, too, "obey your parents in everything, for this pleases the Lord" (Col. 3:20). We do all of it out of submission to Him.

Employers. Workers must "submit to their masters in everything, and to be well-pleasing, not talking back or stealing, but demonstrating utter faithfulness, so that they may adorn the teaching of God our Savior in everything" (Titus 2:9–10). "Whatever you do, do it heartily, as to the Lord and not to men" (Col. 3:23 NKJV). Everything, "as to the Lord." We don't submit to or obey any authority because of *them*, but because of *Him*. Not because *they* are worthy. *He* is worthy!

Church. The leaders He has given you to speak "God's word to you" (Heb. 13:7), you are instructed to "obey" them and "submit to them, since they keep watch over your souls" (v. 17). It's easy for church to become an optional accessory in our lives, as if it's only there to serve and cater to us. No, Christ is the head of the church, and He expects us to honor our spiritual leaders as a way to honor Him.

We obviously cannot submit to an authority that is instructing us to sin or dishonor God. There are solid, biblical grounds for respectful, civil disobedience when leaders demand God's people to sin (Exod. 1:17; Dan. 3:18; 6:10; Acts 5:29). We have a right, even a duty, to appeal to a leader who's not living up to his position or is trying to force us to abandon our primary allegiance to God. Daniel, Esther, and Nehemiah each modeled this. We cannot dishonor God's higher authority to obey their lower authority. In those situations, "we must obey God rather than people" (Acts 5:29).

However, when our authorities are *not* asking us to sin, our job as Christ's disciples is to follow the example of Jesus and respectfully submit to them as unto the Lord. The Bible exhorts us—"first of all"—to pray for them, that "petitions, prayers, intercessions, and thanksgivings be made for everyone, for kings and all those in authority" (1 Tim. 2:1–2). Even the ones we don't like or didn't vote for. It's our job to keep praying for them and asking the Lord to lead them as our leaders. Pagans won't be respecting or praying for them, but believers are the light of the world. Our unexpected respect is a powerful witness and a mind-blowing example to the lost. This is a "good thing" to do that "pleases God our Savior" (v. 3).

All this teaching on authority is solid and true. But in the grip and grind of everyday life, the practical work of respecting and submitting to leaders can be very tough to do. Jesus understands. His cross is proof that He knows what it means—more than we can ever know—to live in submission to an authority whose plans run counter to what our flesh wants and desires.

Today, of course, in resurrected glory, He is seated in heavenly power "far above every ruler and authority, power and dominion, and every title given" (Eph. 1:21). His Father has "put all things under His feet" and has made Him "head over all things to the church" (v. 22 NKJV). But according to Scripture, an incredible day is coming, just before we step into an eternity in His presence, "when he hands over the kingdom to God the Father" (1 Cor. 15:24), when He who rules over every authority today turns and submits to authority Himself.

Keep that picture in mind as you seek to live as His devoted disciple. Jesus never demands anything of you that He hasn't done or isn't doing Himself. Show your family, your friends, your neighbors, your coworkers, how a person surrendered to Christ lives and humbly serves under the authorities of the day. Show them the difference His authority makes in your life.

Father, I acknowledge that all authority comes to us from You. I ask that You would use me as a respectful and supportive example of Jesus in how I prayerfully submit to the biblical, governmental, family, and employment authorities that You have placed over my life. I do it in obedience to Your Word and Your will as a demonstration of my submission to You. Use those in authority over me to guide me, protect me, encourage me, and help me so I may do Your will more completely. In the name of Jesus. Amen.

Going Deeper

Daniel 1:8–16 • Romans 13:1–7 • Titus 3:1

41

Living a Life of Grace

What should His grace inspire me to do?

The law was given through Moses; grace and truth came through Jesus Christ. John 1:17

It's easy to think of grace only in terms of salvation. And when we do, what greater expression of grace can we contemplate! Our sins deserve God's wrath. Our rejection of Him calls for His rejection of us. The fair reward for all our selfish rebellion against Him would be a life separated from Him and from His blessed presence forever.

But grace. By His grace we are saved.

Grace is unmerited favor. Undeserved lovingkindness. Unearned generosity flowing out of a cheerful, giving heart. Grace is seen in the smile of a loving Father delighting in His beloved son or daughter. Grace means that our salvation "is not from yourselves; it is God's gift—not from works, so that no one can boast" (Eph. 2:8–9). And since a believing faith in Christ is our sole contribution into "this grace in which we stand," the only thing we can "boast" about is the glory of the God who's given us His amazing grace to start with (Rom. 5:2).

The appropriate response to being given grace is simply *gratitude*. "Thanks be to God for his indescribable gift!" (2 Cor. 9:15; Luke 17:15). Thanksgiving is actually rooted in the word *grace*. Gratefulness is the gracious fruit that is given back after someone properly receives grace.

The gift of God's saving grace, so incredibly undeserved, is simply to be humbly received. Received and enjoyed. Received and shared. The cheerful giver has brought cheer to the receiver. Just as we would never want someone to resist a gift that we'd purchased and given them, or even try to pay us for it, God gives us grace out of His own loving heart because He wants us to have it, receive it, and enjoy it. Because He is the Lord, "a compassionate and gracious God" (Exod. 34:6).

But grace is hardly a once-in-a-lifetime gift. As believers, we exist and live every day by the grace of God. We're invited at any moment to "approach the throne of grace with boldness, so that we may receive mercy and find grace to help us in time of need" (Heb. 4:16). In every place where we are weak and unsure of ourselves, God's grace is "sufficient" for us (2 Cor. 12:9). "The LORD God is a sun and shield; the LORD gives grace and glory; He withholds no good thing from those who walk with integrity" (Ps. 84:11 NASB). Give Him thanks for His grace! All He has given is "to the praise of his glorious grace" (Eph. 1:6).

If not for God's grace, we would still be under the law. What's the difference between these two? It's the difference between earning wages and receiving a gift. "The wages of sin is death," the Bible says—that's the law—"but the gift of God is eternal life in Christ Jesus our Lord" (Rom. 6:23). That's grace.

His death on the cross demonstrated both. He first shed His blood as a spotless sacrifice, having fulfilled the perfect standards of the law. His death paid our due wage. It satisfied the law's righteous requirement for justice. Sin must be paid for. Jesus paid it all, using the highest currency on earth, His own blood.

But then grace. His death is also for us. The grace of the cross. God in His lovingkindness applies the perfectly paid-up righteousness of Christ to anyone who receives Him as Lord and Savior. Our obligation to the law has been satisfied in Jesus, making us fully accepted by our Father in heaven, as if we'd been following His law without fail all along. We are saved by and can now live on Christ's merits, not our own. We are free to function by His grace, bearing neither guilt nor shame. In Him, "grace and truth" are perfectly joined together (John 1:17; Ps. 85:10). We have nothing to fear because we've been given His righteousness and are pure and blameless in the eyes of heaven.

Can you believe that? You *have* believed that. Receive it with gratefulness!

And so there's nothing to keep any of us from being portraits of grace every day in all our interactions with others. We are called to extend to others the same open-handed grace we've been given. As Jesus said, "Freely you received, freely give" (Matt. 10:8). God has made "every grace overflow to you, so that in every way, always having everything you need, you may excel in every good work . . . enriched in every way for all generosity" (2 Cor. 9:8, 11).

That's why Jesus could teach such radical concepts as turning the other cheek and walking the second mile. If someone wants to "take away your shirt, let him have your coat as well" (Matt. 5:40). "Give to the one who asks you, and don't turn away from the one who wants to borrow from you" (v. 42). Because if we've been freed from the law, if we live now by grace, why hold the rigid demands of the law over the heads of anyone else any longer? Be generous!

Be like Jesus. Speak "gracious words" (Luke 4:22). "Love your enemies and pray for those who persecute you" (Matt. 5:44). Show undeserved compassion. Model patience. Share with extravagant liberality. Be eager to forgive and to keep on forgiving—"seventy times seven" if necessary (Matt. 18:22). Grace doesn't keep score and require justice. That's what law does. End the practice of requiring people to earn any good things you do for them. Show them the same mercy your heavenly Father has shown to you. You cannot out-give God.

"Even sinners love those who love them," Jesus said (Luke 6:32). They don't acknowledge the grace of God already given to them, not even His sustaining grace that gives them air in their lungs and a brilliant sun overhead. So they have no rationale for giving grace to others. But Jesus invites us into the river with Him, where we swim in His undeserved grace every day. Here we rest and receive, experience victory over our sins, and enjoy abiding relationship with the living King of glory. Here our prayers are not just words, lost in a cosmic void, but are willingly heard by our Father in heaven and woven into His plan for us. Here the Lord blesses and protects us, makes His face to shine upon us, looks on us with favor, and gives us peace because of His gracious love toward us (Num. 6:24–26).

And here the same grace that flows from His throne flows through our lives into others' lives. The grace that keeps giving keeps us giving. The grace that saves our souls puts a brightness in our eyes and a noticeable sparkle to our countenance. Do people deserve us to deal so graciously with them? Of course they don't. But then again, neither do we. That's why it's called grace!

Father, I thank You for Your grace! I praise You for being so gracious! Help me live in the humble awareness that I've done nothing to earn what You have done for me. It is all because of Your grace. So shine Your grace through me. Make it so visible on my face that others will know I've been changed by a loving and kind God. Give me an opportunity in the days ahead to put Your grace into practice, to unexpectedly bless others without cost in Christ's name. Amen.

Going Deeper

Matthew 5:38–45 • Romans 5:12–21 • Ephesians 4:29

42

Living a Life of Forgiveness

Why must I forgive others' offenses?

"Forgive us our debts, as we also have forgiven our debtors." Matthew 6:12

The model prayer Jesus gave us is a daily prayer. It teaches us to worship daily, submit to God daily, and seek His provision and His protection daily. "Give us this day our daily bread" (Matt. 6:11 NASB). That's what we want. Always abiding in Him, receiving what we need from Him. Every day!

But consider this. His prayer also reveals another everyday expectation: to daily forgive everyone who sins against us. "Forgive us our debts, as we forgive our debtors" (Matt. 6:12 NKJV). Staying right with God includes staying right in how we respond to others. Since the Lord has given us complete forgiveness and heaven by His grace, everyone who wrongs us should now receive our grace and forgiveness too.

Jesus is asking us to stop keeping score or operating by the law. To stop holding on to emotional debts. To stop requiring others to somehow pay for what they've done. We live by grace now. We also extend His grace to others, regardless of who they are.

The Bible is clear, we will be wronged in life. "Offenses will certainly come" (Luke 17:1). But anytime we don't work through our hurt and anger, refusing to forgive, we are then sinning too. Creating more offenses. Operating in pride and self-righteousness. Worse, we are assuming rights we don't possess by exalting ourselves onto the judgment seat.

This is where the heart of a devoted disciple shifts gears. We are willing to die to ourselves. Remembering who we are in Christ. Defaulting to the example of the Lord we follow.

Forgiving like Jesus. Which was how? On the cross. Dying to Himself. Forgiving all.

Think about it. For any of us to spend an eternity in God's holy presence in heaven, we need 100 percent of our sins forgiven—not even one infraction unresolved. Thank God the cross of Jesus is complete. The Father has provided us total forgiveness at the loving expense of Christ's death. Praise God for His grace! We are completely reliant upon it. Undeserved grace.

So now it's our turn as His disciples. To be like Jesus. This is a test.

If we refuse to extend this same grace to others, we are imposing on them a standard that God has not imposed on us. Because if He had, it's an eternal burden we couldn't survive.

We are demanding someone else be judged by the weight of God's law, while, at the same time, expecting God's grace for ourselves. Justice for them. Mercy for us.

We're not saying you shouldn't grieve and feel strong emotions when others sin against you. Sinners sin, and it's wrong, and it hurts. We're not saying you shouldn't confront the person in love and humility and help lead them to repentance (Matt. 18:15–16; Luke 17:3). But regardless of what they do, you must still turn it all over to the Lord, the righteous Judge, and release the anger from your heart. Letting Him handle it from there (Rom. 12:17–19).

Any other approach is only inviting more sin and bringing grief to the Holy Spirit (Eph. 4:30–32). Not forgiving is not an option. Besides, not forgiving is really bad for you. Going to bed angry becomes bitterness inside your heart, which is a "root" problem that causes countless other problems (Heb. 12:15).

Physically. Bitterness is toxic to the body. It affects your sleep, tightens your neck, hardens your facial expressions, and lowers your resistance to disease. The grudges and angry resentments you harbor inside do not go away. They fester and poison from within. Draining you emotionally.

Socially. Watch bitter people, and you'll consistently see them hijack conversations, redirecting any subject into an opportunity to express all the pain they've suffered and the hurt they still feel. Always the victim. Rather than keep the damage contained, they spread slander and accusations around, causing others to think badly of the sinner they're reporting on. Devaluing them now in more hearts. And possibly causing the listeners to make a note to avoid this slanderer who is clearly bitter and spreads venom so freely.

Spiritually. Here is where the effect of bitterness is most severe. It hinders our fellowship with God, causing us to feel distant from Him. The Spirit is grieved. Abiding is obstructed. Our worshiping and our praying become dry. Our joy fades. No peace. Our love for God and others becomes a legalistic chore instead of a continual blessing from grace-filled hearts.

Bitterness also gives Satan "opportunity" to gain ground in your head and heart (Eph. 4:26–27). He's an accuser, remember? He will incite you to harbor cold, hateful feelings toward the person who hurt you. He will foster an attitude of self-pity at the unfairness of it all. He will plant confusing doubts that question God's goodness. And know this: when Satan is involved, it will not be just a passing thought but an ongoing, dark loop that keeps droning on repeatedly. Distracting your day and keeping you up at night.

Listen to Jesus' epic answer to all this: "Whenever you stand praying, if you have anything against anyone, forgive him, so that your Father in heaven will also forgive you your wrongdoing" (Mark 11:25). Get all of it out. Now! Today! Never let the condition of your heart be dependent on what others do or have done.

We know it can feel almost wrong to forgive, as if it's unjust to let something go that's so obviously against God's will and His Word. And it *would* be unjust if we were God. Like we've said, the only reason He's justified in forgiving us is because His Son lived and died as a perfect sacrifice. But because He did—because we are so completely forgiven—we are not in a position of being unforgiving ourselves. God is judge. He's on it.

It's past time to release the debt and let this go.

Do you have anyone you need to forgive? Anything against anyone from your past? Any suffering that has haunted you and still depresses you? Any dark hurt stuffed deep down inside that you've tried to pretend is gone? Healing doesn't begin until forgiveness takes place. It's time to take it all to the cross, lay it before the blood-stained feet of Jesus, and leave all the pain and hurt there for Him to handle from this day onward.

Fully extend the grace that God has extended to you. Yes, it's undeserved. But nobody deserves grace. Including you. It's only given. We dare you to pray the prayer below and move on into total victory today. Please let today be the day!

Our Father in heaven, holy is Your name. May Your kingdom come; may Your will be done in my life today. Please forgive me of all my sins, specifically sins of anger, judgment, unforgiveness, and resentment. Thank You for the cross and Your forgiveness. Because of it, I choose now to extend Your grace and fully forgive each and every person who's sinned against me in the past, especially ________________ (name them). I fully release them now over to You and release my anger and hurt against them completely. They now owe me nothing. I pray You would cleanse any bitterness and anger out of my life. Take back any ground I've given over to Satan and fill me with Your Holy Spirit. Help me walk daily in Your grace and forgiveness. Help me stay hard to offend and quick to forgive. Love my enemies through me, I pray, in Jesus' name. Amen.

Going Deeper

Matthew 18:21–35 • Hebrews 12:14–15 • 1 Peter 2:19–25

43

Living a Life of Love

How does a disciple walk in love?

"By this everyone will know that you are my disciples, if you love one another." John 13:35

God is love. And all He does flows out of all He is. When we realize Jesus is motivated by love, it changes how we view His decisions, receive His words, and submit to His commands.

He is *for* us, not against us.

The love that Jesus modeled throughout His ministry was not the world's fickle, performance-based love, a love that keeps score and must be earned. Many children grow up in homes where they only get attention or affection when they behave or perform. As adults, they tend to assume God's love is the same way, that it must be earned by their good deeds, by jumping through religious hoops. Then when they do something wrong, they naturally feel like they can't receive God's love and forgiveness because they don't deserve it.

But God's love is not for sale and is never earned. It is freely given. He loves us when we are walking in righteousness, and He loves us when we are stumbling in sin, so that He can lead us *out* of our sins, away from the things that are destroying us. "God proves his own love for us in that while we were still sinners, Christ died for us" (Rom. 5:8)—even when we were His enemies, rejecting Him, rebelling against Him. And we can do the same for others.

How? By remembering what God's love is like.

God's love "bears all things, believes all things, hopes all things, endures all things" (1 Cor. 13:7). It never quits or fails. Harsh circumstances do not stop this kind of love. They reveal it. The Bible describes God's perfect love as being "patient" and "kind" (v. 4).

Patience is love on the defense. It can endure and overcome evil. Patience means being "slow to anger" (Ps. 103:8). Longsuffering. Not easily irritated. Hard to offend and quick to forgive. Patience gives people breathing room. Permission to be human. More time to grow.

Kindness is love on the offense. It helps us initiate and maximize good things. Kindness is where love meets needs and blesses others without being asked or forced. It is gentle, compassionate, and does not require a reward or demand recognition.

This is the love He calls each of us to live out in our relationships. "I give you a new command," He told His disciples: "Love one another. Just as I have loved you, you are also to love one another" (John 13:34). The more like Christ we become, the more loving, faithful, and hopeful we become toward others.

The more we walk with Him, abide in Him, and obey His commands, the more our capacity to love will grow (1 John 5:2; 3:23–24).

God's love is not based upon the one being loved but the one choosing to love. He does not love us because we're so lovable but because He's so loving. It's His nature. As water is wet and fire is hot, God is love. When we realize and humbly receive the love of God for us and what Jesus willingly endured for us, He fills our tanks and satisfies our souls so that we can love others the way He loves us. The apostle Paul prayed for believers' eyes to be opened so they could realize the vast greatness of God's love for them (Eph. 3:14–19). Fueled by His love, we can then love anyone and everyone, whether friends, neighbors, family, or enemies.

God's Spirit is the source of God's love in us and through us. Truly loving others is impossible apart from God's help (1 John 4:7–9). We can't manufacture perfect love out of our own sinful hearts. But at salvation, we become God's beloved children. "Beloved" is our new identity. God then places His Spirit in us, and His love is the first fruit of His Spirit (Gal. 5:22). He freely pours out His love into our hearts (Rom. 5:5). This enables us to love others with God's selfless love, to "be imitators of God, as dearly loved children," able to "walk in love, as Christ also loved us and gave himself for us" (Eph. 5:1–2).

God's love leads us to pursue God's best for others in every area of their lives. Consider this prayer: "Beloved, I pray that in all respects you may prosper and be in good health, just as your soul prospers" (3 John 2 NASB). This verse reveals the beautiful heart and hope of love. God's love cares holistically about others—their health, their marriage, their family, their faith, their finances, their future. It makes us want them to experience

God's best in every area, starting with salvation, then leading to the abundant life Jesus came to give them (John 10:10). Love doesn't just feel emotions. It drives us to get busy, get involved, and get our hands dirty. Never by supporting someone in their sin but by truly wanting them at peace with God. We may help someone out of a literal ditch, but our real goal is to help them fully experience the gospel, God's Word, Christ's love, and a genuine walk with Jesus—His best for their lives. Ultimately heaven!

God's love simplifies life and solves problems. How can you have a better marriage and family? Better friendships? Better work relationships? *Focus on loving people.* How can you live with fewer regrets? Make the best use of your time? *Focus on loving people.* One of the best ways to bring clarity to disputes and solve complicated disagreements is by simply asking, "What would love do in this situation?"

As God's Spirit gives you a growing love for others, you will increasingly view people as having priceless worth, knowing that God created them in His image and Jesus died for them on the cross. You'll quit focusing on their sins but compassionately on their needs. That's how Jesus viewed the helpless crowds who approached Him and the heartless soldiers who crucified Him (Matt. 14:14; Luke 23:34).

So consider *love* the new focus of your faith. Following Jesus is not about religion. It is a genuine love relationship with God and with others. When you walk in God's love, you naturally do what He says (Matt. 22:36–40). You avoid sin simply by focusing on loving God and others each day. Sin is the opposite of love. It grieves and quenches the Spirit's work in you (Eph. 4:30–32). But His love flows freely through you as you keep abiding in Him, repenting of any unforgiveness or hidden sin in your life, and walking in obedience to Jesus.

Every disciple of Jesus Christ should be a flowing channel of God's love. He has called us to this. It is the pinnacle of spiritual maturity (2 Pet. 1:5–8). He's invited us to abide and walk in His love—a love that is unselfish, unconditional, and unstoppable. What a privilege! "May the Lord cause you to increase and overflow with love for one another, and for everyone, just as we do for you" (1 Thess. 3:12).

Heavenly Father, I pray You will open our eyes to Your great love for us. Cleanse our hearts from anything that hinders Your love. Satisfy us with the love of Jesus and make us channels of love by the power of Your Spirit. Love others through us, Lord! May we walk in the fullness of Your love for us, and may others be richly blessed by our love for them! In Jesus' name. Amen.

Going Deeper

Romans 13:8–10 • 1 Corinthians 13 • Colossians 3:12–14

44

Living a Life of Worship

What does a worshiping life look like?

"An hour is coming, and is now here, when the true worshipers will worship the Father in Spirit and in truth. Yes, the Father wants such people to worship him." John 4:23

Worshiping is what people do. All day, every day. They may not realize it, but all of their lives, words, thinking, and service is orbiting around what they prioritize the most.

What are *we* worshiping? Devoting ourselves to the Lord is what true followers of Jesus do. He becomes number one in our hearts and lives.

This aligns with God's perspective. The Bible says Jesus is "before all things, and by him all things hold together. He is also the head of the body, the church; he is the beginning, the firstborn from the dead, so that he might come to have first place in everything" (Col. 1:17–18).

First place in everything. Not just Sunday things. All things. Everything in our lives is meant to orbit around Him, around the one our hearts need and love the most. "In Him we live and move and have our being" (Acts 17:28 NASB).

So never limit worshiping to the church service on Sunday morning. That's a small part of your worship. Worshiping together with other believers at church is so important, but individual worship can happen all day long, everywhere you go. In your heart, with your words. With your prayers. With your attitude. With your work. With all of you.

"From the rising of the sun to its setting, let the name of the LORD be praised" (Ps. 113:3). And the night shift takes over after that!—"all you servants of the LORD, who stand by night in the house of the LORD! Lift up your hands to the holy place and bless the LORD!" (Ps. 134:1–2 ESV).

Does this level of worship sound extreme? Hopefully so. Because it is.

It's the wholehearted kind of love and adoration that Mary, the sister of Lazarus, once poured out on Jesus in His presence (Mark 14:3–9; John 12:1–8). It was less than a week before He would be tortured and crucified. He'd been invited to a dinner where suddenly the fragrance of fine perfume filled the air, permeating the whole house. Mary willingly poured an entire jar of very expensive spikenard oil on Jesus' feet. People were shocked. "Why wasn't this perfume sold for three hundred denarii and given to the poor?" (John 12:5). *What a waste of precious resources,* they thought. Haven't we sometimes thought the same thing—considering our time and money too precious to "waste" on worship, our schedule too crowded to make room for worship in it? But Jesus rebuked them. They did not love Him like she did. "Leave her alone. Why do you trouble her? She has done a beautiful thing to me" (Mark 14:6 ESV).

Beautiful worship. Isn't that what you want your worship to be? The kind that gets God's attention? The kind He's delighted to receive? Not like the people of Malachi's day, who brought God their second-best in worship. "'Am I to accept that from your hands?' asks the LORD" (Mal. 1:13). Your leftovers? The least amount of worship you can bring? The bare minimum so you don't feel guilty?

Look around during a church service and ask yourself if people are greatly pouring out their hearts in worship or are acting like it's a waste of their precious time. Do they seem grumpy or grateful? Tender or calloused? Motivated or mentally asleep? Are they giving their worship generously or reluctantly?

But save the longest look for yourself. What kind of worship does the Lord see flowing out of *your* life? Is it beautiful, or is it kind of boring? Do you get more excited about sports or about spiritual things? Worship music or secular music? Serving God or serving yourself? Oh, Lord, please forgive us!

Does He not deserve our all? All our worship? "You are worthy, O Lord, to receive glory and honor and power; for You created all things, and by Your will they exist and were created" (Rev. 4:11 NKJV). Walk slowly through this verse again. He is *worthy*. And He is *Lord*, our supreme authority. Worthy to receive *glory*, to be recognized for who He truly is. To receive *honor*, our most valuable sacrifice of praise. And to receive *power*, our continued awe and wonder. He is better than all. Greater than all.

To give this abundance of worship to anyone or anything else is to break the first commandment, where God told His people to "have no other gods before Me" (Exod. 20:3 NASB). We are His people today, saved for "the praise of his glorious grace" (Eph. 1:6). And we respond to His grace by wholeheartedly obeying what Jesus called the "greatest and most important" commandment: "Love the Lord your God with all your heart, with all your soul, and with all your mind" (Matt. 22:37–38).

Worshiping Him. First and most above all.

If someone were to record our conversations, track our spending, monitor our time and calendar, and catalog our entertainment choices, the raw data would tell a lot. It would tell the real story of what we actually love and live for the most. Where our daily *worship* actually goes. It would tell us what we get the most excited about, what we sacrifice the most for. What we prioritize above other things. It might show us if our hearts love the Lord or an idol.

"For it is written, As I live, says the Lord, every knee will bow to me, and every tongue will give praise to God" (Rom. 14:11). As human beings, we've been given the highest form of intelligence on earth. We've been given the greatest capacity to use language, music, service, and all our resources for something important. Is there anything more worthy of it all than our God? Most of all, we've been given the greatest reason for praise of all—the gift of Jesus coming and dying for us and then being raised from the dead for the glory of God the Father.

So the next time you see a spectacular sunset, lift your heart in praise to God. The next time you're wowed by a scientific discovery or a fascinating thought about the incredible design of creation, turn your amazement into a worshiping moment. Praise Him with "joy unspeakable and full of glory" (1 Pet. 1:8 KJV).

And the next time you enter into prayer—which we hope will be immediately after you finish reading this chapter—fill it with sincere praise for who He is. Fill it with overflowing gratitude for what He's done for you, even today. "Praise God in his sanctuary," but also "praise him in his mighty expanse" (Ps. 150:1), anywhere you happen to be, at any part of your day. "Praise him for his powerful acts; praise him for his abundant greatness" (v. 2).

If you're not sure whether it's a good time to worship, whether silent or aloud, public or private, with your hands or with your lips, with your time or with your resources, the answer is always an overflowing yes. Yes to all of the above.

And if you're not sure whether you're that kind of person or not, just check to see if you're breathing and if your heart is beating. "Let everything that has breath praise the LORD" (v. 6 NKJV).

It's time to worship. It is always time to worship.

Father, I worship You. You are worthy of all my praise. I lift Your name above all others. I acknowledge You as being more wonderful, more amazing, more loving, more pure and holy than I can even imagine. Thank You for saving me. Thank You for forgiving my sin. Thank You for making me a new person and promising me an eternity with You. I love You. I praise You. In the name of Jesus. Amen.

Going Deeper

Psalm 119:164 • Matthew 11:25–26 • Hebrews 13:15

45

Living a Life of Generosity

How much giving does God expect of me?

"Freely you received, freely give." Matthew 10:8

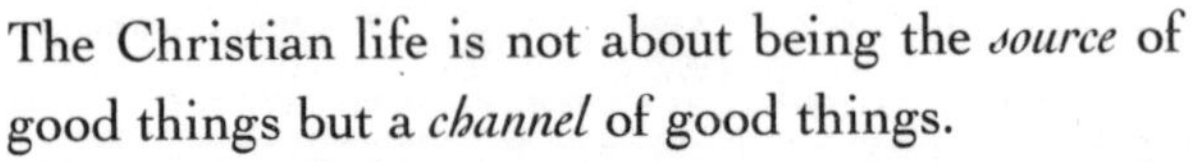

The Christian life is not about being the *source* of good things but a *channel* of good things.

Jesus modeled this dynamic. He graciously humbled Himself, became poor for our sakes, and emptied Himself to be human in every way. At His baptism, He received the Father's loving blessing and the indwelling of the Holy Spirit. Then, by the Spirit's power, Jesus served the ongoing needs of those around Him. He relied on the same wells of supply that God graciously makes available to us through Christ (Phil. 4:19; Eph. 1:3–19).

Read the Gospels and watch the flow. Jesus was constantly praying to and receiving from His Father. He was led by and receiving power from the Holy Spirit. Most surprising of all, He received practical aid and support from other people (Luke 8:3). He graciously blessed them while humbly allowing them to bless Him. As a man, He freely leaned on the fellowship, service, and generosity of others who followed Him. From all these streams, He walked in a steady flow of infilling and outpouring. Loving and being loved. Serving and being served. Always bearing fruit. Ready for every good work.

Jesus stepped into each day full of the love of His Father, full of the power and wisdom of the Spirit, and freely sharing whatever He had, wherever He went, however it was needed. This was His lifestyle. He was a ready servant to others and a fountain of the Father's endless supply.

This is countercultural. Some people struggle to give. They are like walking drains, only receiving. Their lives grow stagnant like the Dead Sea. They strangle the outflow of resources. Consuming. Hoarding. Souring. Daily squandering opportunities to generously serve, give, help, and bless others.

Other people, however, are resistant to *receiving*. They stressfully overwork and overserve. Self-reliant and self-sufficient. Not admitting need. But by struggling to rest in the Lord or rely on anyone else, they eventually wear down, run dry, and burn out. They mean well but don't always end well.

The life that Jesus modeled and makes possible for His followers thrives on both giving *and* receiving. We take in; we pour out. He said, "If anyone is thirsty, let him come to me and drink. The one who believes in me, as the Scripture has said, will have streams of living water flow from deep within him." He was talking about the Holy Spirit, whom "those who believed in Jesus were going to receive" (John 7:37–39).

If we want to become a fountain of living water, we must first believe the gospel. We *receive* His Spirit and His forgiveness. Then as we daily abide in Christ and humbly open our hearts to receive all good things by the Lord's grace and from others, this increase of inflow overflows in *giving*. Then as we generously give and share, we find ourselves "enriched in every way for all generosity" (2 Cor. 9:11). It's like the rain cycle. Our supply is continually replenished.

As a channel of God's blessings, what specific things should we daily receive and freely give? Here is a starter list:

Receive and share LOVE. "As the Father has loved me," Jesus said, "I have also loved you. Remain in my love" (John 15:9). The amazing love Jesus shared in the Gospels was the overflow of love He constantly received from His Father. This is the secret to loving others—daily receiving God's love for us personally and then pouring it back out on Him and others. "This is my command: Love one another *as I have loved you*" (John 15:12, emphasis added). As you daily look to the cross, as you read about God's love in His Word, and as you pray for His Spirit to fill you with love (Rom. 5:5), you'll be able to rest in His love and share it with God and others. Here's a great prayer to pray: "Thank You for loving me, Lord. Please fill me and make me a channel of Your love to others!"

Receive and share TRUTH. There's no need to be a self-made genius or try to impress others with your brilliance. Just continually seek wisdom, understanding, counsel, and knowledge—from the Lord, from His Word, from His Spirit, and from others. At the same time, prayerfully share what God's been teaching you. As Paul said to Timothy, "What you have heard from me in the presence of many witnesses, commit to faithful men who will be able to teach others also" (2 Tim. 2:2).

By receiving and sharing truth that the Lord supplies, you are blessed and a blessing through the Word of God. Are you in the Word daily? Are you also sharing with others what you're learning? Then "thanks be to God, who . . . manifests through us the sweet aroma of the knowledge of Him in every place" (2 Cor. 2:14 NASB).

Receive and share CORRECTION. Part of walking in truth is experiencing the sharpening of God's Word and staying teachable and accountable to one another. Wise believers freely receive and give helpful correction. It doesn't need to be loud or rude and may sometimes feel awkward, but love can do awkward. Jesus freely corrected His followers in love. "One who rebukes a person will later find more favor than the one who flatters with his tongue" (Prov. 28:23).

Receive and share COMFORT. When we suffer as believers, God comforts us and may send others to encourage us as we grieve. As we receive this comfort, God enables us to then comfort others. "Blessed be the God and Father of our Lord Jesus Christ, the Father of mercies and the God of all comfort. He comforts us in all our affliction." That's the *receiving* part. "So that we may be able to comfort those who are in any kind of affliction, through the comfort we ourselves receive from God" (2 Cor. 1:3–4). That's the *giving* part. Both are so needed!

Receive and share RESOURCES. God "richly provides us with all things to enjoy" (1 Tim. 6:17). He has a rich river of supply. We should work hard and provide for our own needs but also willingly receive any financial blessings and gifts with humility and gratitude. Likewise, we must keep committing "to do what is good, to be rich in good works, to be generous and willing to share." This is how Christ's followers support ministry, missions, one another, and store up "treasure for themselves as a good foundation for the coming age, so that they may take hold of what is truly life" (1 Tim. 6:18–19). God loves a cheerful giver!

All believers should be loving channels of overflowing generosity.

Receiving gratefully and giving graciously.

So keep growing, keep sowing, and keep His flow going!

Father, I praise You, the creator and source of all good things. We are empty without You. I pray You would open our hearts and minds to freely receive from Your hand and Your Holy Spirit, then to freely give back to You and others on a daily basis. Make us rivers of blessings and fountains of Your love, grace, and resources. In Jesus' name. Amen.

Going Deeper

Leviticus 19:9–10 • 2 Corinthians 9:6–15 •
Philippians 4:18–20

46

Living a Life of Compassion

Where is my heart most needed today?

When he saw the crowds, he felt compassion for them, because they were distressed and dejected, like sheep without a shepherd. Matthew 9:36

Showing concern and compassion to someone who is greatly suffering is one of the most powerful demonstrations of the love of Christ in this world. It's also an eye-opening witness to nonbelievers. On the other hand, being insensitive and uncaring to the pain of others can deepen the hurt, become a stumbling block to the gospel, and drive people away from our Savior.

Compassion. It starts with seeing genuine need and literally feeling something in your gut. It's the response of a tender heart.

You feel pity, concern, sympathy, and even affection for those who are hurting and suffering. When you feel it, it's motivating.

Calloused hearts turn away, but tender hearts step in closer and must do something. The need *moves* us into compassion. Action. We must go to them. Enter their pain. Show them some type of gentleness and kindness, in whatever way is appropriate. We share in their suffering. We seek to somehow lessen the burden or meet the need they're experiencing. We look, we listen, we comfort, we serve, we give. "How can I help?" "What can I do?" "I'm so sorry for what you're going through." "I care about you." *This is the tender heart of compassion.*

Jesus was and is the master of compassion. As God, He "forgives all your iniquity; he heals all your diseases. He redeems your life from the Pit; he crowns you with faithful love and compassion" (Ps. 103:3–4). And as man, when He was living on the earth, He tenderly personified compassion. He walked it and talked it. No one was ever a more compassionate person.

Instead of being irritated or disgusted by the stressed-out crowds, His heart was *moved* by them, by knowing the hard-traveled burdens and the hurt behind their eyes. "He felt compassion for them"—even though He could so easily have overlooked them. Or considered them an interruption. Or worried how He was going to make His next appointment, with all these people now looking to Him, wanting something from Him, taking up so many hours of His time.

Who did Jesus demonstrate tenderhearted compassion toward?

He had compassion on the weary. Like so many people today, the crowds in Matthew 9 were "distressed and dejected" (v. 36). Tired and discouraged. Beat up, overloaded, and worn out. Exhausted just from the effort it took to live. Jesus felt it and cared for them. And as His followers, we too should recognize when those around us are getting weary. We should recognize the fatigue on their faces. Look around and you'll see it. What would Jesus do about it? Follow His lead.

He had compassion on the untaught. In Mark's version of this same event, he added one detail. After feeling compassion for the crowd, Jesus "began to teach them many things" (Mark 6:34). One of the main reasons people avoid church, especially any type of Bible study or class, is the fear of being asked a question they can't answer. Jesus didn't look down on people who were ignorant. Instead He patiently taught them. Not in fancy, lofty language but using the words and analogies that connected well with the common people. How do you treat people who are less educated or understanding than you? Do you avoid them or help them?

He had compassion on the grieving. Once while approaching a local town, Jesus saw a funeral procession coming out of the city gate. A mother, already widowed, was now mourning the loss of her only son, doubling her grief. "When the Lord saw her, he had compassion on her" (Luke 7:13). His heart broke for her, seeing her weeping. Even though He had power over death and could raise people back to life, first "Jesus wept" with those experiencing the trauma of death (John 11:35). Not from a distance but with His tender presence.

He had compassion on the disorganized. As thousands of people were growing hungry, Jesus took His disciples to one side to show them how His mind worked. These crowds had gotten way out of town, late in the day, unprepared for the night or the journey home. "I have compassion on the crowd," Jesus said to His disciples as He prepared to feed the people (Mark 8:2).

How do we respond to the disorganized and irresponsible? Do we lift our nose or extend our hands?

Even in His parables, Jesus was the compassionate character at the center.

He had compassion on the poor. In His parable about forgiveness in Matthew 18, Jesus was the sympathetic king whose servant begged for more time to pay off a debt. "The master of that servant had compassion, released him, and forgave him the loan" (v. 27). How might God allow you to leverage your authority over finances to lessen the suffering of others?

He had compassion on the victim. The story of the good Samaritan is one of the greatest examples of compassion in history (Luke 10:25–37). While two people kept the wounded man at a safe distance, the Samaritan looked at his need, felt compassion, and went into action. He had every reason not to do anything, but he greatly inconvenienced himself, demonstrating loving compassion in multiple ways.

But this is our Jesus. The story is really about Him. He looked on us with compassion, just as He looked on the blind, on the lame, on the leper, on the deaf. He saw us in need of forgiveness. He moved toward us in love. He stretched out His arms in compassion and took on our suffering to bear our greatest burdens. He gives us so much grace! "Compassion and forgiveness belong to the Lord our God" (Dan. 9:9–10). That's the God we serve.

A key reason people do not show compassion is lack of proximity. Like the priest in that story who walked by on the other side of the road, it's easy to stay at a comfortable distance from people who are hurting, never inviting anyone close or stepping in to see or identify any real needs. Even if their need becomes known, it's easy to avoid doing anything about it.

Jesus didn't camp out in the synagogues; He went to the people. To their towns and streets. To their markets and homes. To their needs. Close enough to look them in the eyes, feel their pain with them, and serve them. And because He did this so often, Jesus was never without opportunity for showing love and changing lives by His loving compassion.

As children of God who are devoted to Jesus, we must prayerfully get out of our comfort zones and intentionally go to people. Close enough and long enough to show them the compassion of Christ. Asking people "How are you doing?" "How can I pray for you?" "How can I help you?" Being willing. Modeling the beauty of the gospel that has shown us so much compassion.

What is a practical step you can take in the next few days to shine the compassion of Christ to someone who is in great need right now?

Father, I thank You for daily bearing my burdens and meeting my needs. Please give me Your eyes and Your heart to see practical ways so I can show Your love to others. Grow compassion in me. Make my heart more tender. Make my tears flow freely. Make me more like Jesus. Bear the burdens of others through me. In Christ's name I pray. Amen.

Going Deeper

Psalm 25:6–7 • Mark 1:39–42 • 1 John 3:16–18

47

LIVING A LIFE OF SERVICE

WHY IS SERVING SO IMPORTANT?

"The Son of Man did not come to be served, but to serve, and to give his life as a ransom for many." Matthew 20:28

Jesus' twelve disciples had gone from being ordinary nobodies to personal friends of the Messiah. They were also handpicked for His inner circle. They must have had moments thinking they were really moving up in the world, because they kept debating among themselves "who should be considered the greatest" (Luke 22:24).

But when Jesus noticed this foolish tendency, He used it as an opportunity to explain to them what greatness actually looks like in God's eyes. The one who is truly great, whom God makes great, is the one who humbly chooses to serve. To be the servant of others.

Scripture reveals that human self-exaltation is an empty pursuit in God's kingdom. True disciples are those who get over themselves and willingly dive in to serve others. Like Jesus did.

Imagine what went through their minds when He said, "Whoever wants to become great among you must be your servant" (Matt. 20:26). That's not what they wanted to hear. They might have been thinking: *Was He saying being a servant is what we're supposed to be striving for? That's the opposite of the plan. We're moving up, not stepping down. What planet is He from?*

He's from heaven. Where serving is what God does all the time. Where the divine members of the Trinity serve each other constantly. Not out of forced obligation but out of an outpouring of deep, genuine love.

Because love likes to serve. Respect feels honored to serve. Humility freely serves. Compassion tenderly serves. Kindness graciously serves. Friends joyfully serve.

And disciples serve by following the perfect example of Christ.

In God's economy, those who exalt themselves need to be humbled, and those who humble themselves will be exalted. Embracing your role as the servant of Jesus is a prerequisite to being mightily used by God.

Look at how many times in Scripture someone referred to themselves as a "servant" of Jesus Christ. Paul did (Rom. 1:1). Peter did (2 Pet. 1:1). John did (Rev. 1:1). James did (James 1:1). Jude did (Jude 1). First chapter, first verse, first words out of their mouths. Their identity as the "servant of the Lord" preceded almost everything else.

Abraham, Isaac, and Jacob, the patriarchs of God's people, were first called His "servants" (Exod. 32:13). Moses, the legend from Egypt who guided Israel through the wilderness, was operating as the "servant" of God (Num. 12:7). Joshua, who picked up Moses's mantle, introduced himself as the Lord's "servant" (Josh. 5:14). Ruth chose to be a "servant" to Boaz, who married her (Ruth 3:9). Abigail was a "servant" to David, and he married her too (1 Sam. 25:41). Great prophets were first "servants," including Elijah (1 Kings 18:36), Nehemiah (Neh. 1:11), and Daniel (Dan. 9:17). Mary, the mother of Jesus, said, "I am the Lord's servant" (Luke 1:38).

Even Jesus "emptied himself by assuming the form of a servant" (Phil. 2:7). He served constantly and willingly in every city and situation. Whether it was preaching to masses, dining with the wealthy, healing lepers, or washing nasty feet, Jesus humbly met the need of the moment out of compassion, love, and service.

Observe and learn. When the first line of your job description is "servant of the Lord," you are much more readily prepared to take on any task God lays before you—not just to do it, but to do it better and with a better attitude than you would ever have done it otherwise. A man who's a leader first and a servant later will not be as good of a leader. Or a husband. Or a pastor. Or a plumber. Or a movie producer. We must first see ourselves as servants of Christ, and then all our other roles build upon that foundation.

We must pause here. Our mother, Rhonwyn Kendrick, is this kind of person—one of the greatest servants of the Lord we've ever known. We cannot thank the Lord (or her) enough for everything she's done for us—from pausing her job to raise us at home, to serving our father's ministry, then later his daily medical needs, to preparing countless meals for friends and strangers in her home, to rising early every day to pray for us. Great is her reward in heaven. Everything we do is blessed because of her support and loving willingness to Christ and others. She's been praying for this book as well. Thank you, Mom! We love you so much.

God is always looking for willing servants. Like the patriarchs. Like the apostles. Like Jesus.

Under Old Testament law, when a slave had paid off his debts and was released from formal servitude, if he deeply respected and cared for his master he could return and willingly choose to continue serving—but this time, out of love (Deut. 15:12–17). As servants of Jesus Christ, we've been set free by His blood and are no longer in bondage, whether to sin, the world, or the law. "It was for freedom that Christ set us free" (Gal. 5:1 NASB). But now in our New Testament freedom, realizing what an amazing Savior we've been given to lead us, we gladly come to Him and willingly serve Him and others for the rest of our lives, out of our deep love for Him.

Our servant leader.

The good works that change the world are accomplished by willing servants. Discipleship happens from generation to generation through humble believers willing to serve. "For we are not proclaiming ourselves but Jesus Christ as Lord, and ourselves as your servants for Jesus' sake" (2 Cor. 4:5). Even the spiritual gifts we've been given are intended to help us "to serve others" (1 Pet. 4:10). By thinking and saying, "I'm just here to serve," you can lower your stress level and better step into any situation, more ready to bless and be blessed.

Like the first disciples, our fleshly inclination is to self-promote. We want better treatment at the head table. We want more recognition for who we are and what we've done. But at the judgment, Jesus will honor those who served Him by feeding the hungry, showing hospitality to strangers, serving the various needs of others, and bringing the hope of Christ to the hopeless. As He welcomes us into His presence forever, we will hear Him say those words we've lived our whole lives longing to hear, "Well done, good and faithful servant!" (Matt. 25:21).

May it be so of us. May it be so of you! It's time to serve.

Heavenly Father, we praise You for Your greatness. It is our honor to serve and worship You. Bring to the surface every self-exalting thought and vain motive. Remove them from our hearts. Help us enter each situation with humility and gratitude, wanting only to do whatever brings You the most glory. We are the servants of the Lord. Make us like Jesus, driven by love, and willing to serve those around us in need, in Jesus' name. Amen.

Going Deeper

Matthew 25:37–40 • John 13:14–15 • 1 Corinthians 4:1

PART X

DISCIPLESHIP

How Do I Make Disciples of Others?

48

PRAYING FOR A HARVEST

WHAT IS THE NEXT STEP IN MAKING DISCIPLES?

He said to his disciples, "The harvest is abundant, but the workers are few. Therefore, pray to the Lord of the harvest to send out workers into his harvest." Matthew 9:37–38

Jesus always looked into the eyes of people through an eternal lens. He not only saw their desperation as lost sheep but their priceless value in the eyes of God.

He valued them like a landowner values his fruitful fields almost ready for harvest, covered in beautiful, abundant crops, rapidly ripening on the vine. It's the heart's desire of every farmer—the rich reward from his and his workers' hard, hot hours of plowing, sowing, fertilizing, irrigating, waiting, preparing.

Harvest. A harvest worthy of the price paid to obtain it.

When Jesus looked out on the abundant crowds, that's what He saw. Not rows of ripening grapes or grain, but precious souls, eternal souls, ready to be redeemed. Redeemed into eternal life, to be enjoyed forever, for the glory of the God who made them. Absolutely worth the hard sacrifice of the cross. And well worth the investment and careful attention of the workers.

The Bible says there is coming an ultimate "harvest time" when God, the righteous judge, will be seeking "fruit from the vineyard" (Luke 20:10). All heaven is preparing to collect this harvest. The souls of those whom Christ died to save. To redeem and rescue their lives so that none of them are wasted.

Yes, this harvest is abundant and ripening. "Open your eyes," Jesus said to His disciples, "and look at the fields, because they are ready for harvest. The reaper is already receiving pay and gathering fruit for eternal life, so that the sower and reaper can rejoice together" (John 4:35–36).

But He also pointed out a problem: "The harvest is abundant, but the workers are few" (Matt. 9:37). There weren't enough people waking up and showing up to work the fields. There were only these twelve men with Jesus at the moment. How could so few carry out so much?

"Pray to the Lord of the harvest" (Matt. 9:38). Before He told them to go, He told them to pray. See the needs, then fall on your knees. Because before you can *reap* a harvest, there must *be* a harvest. Lots of intentional preparation. The first step of spiritual soil preparation is the excellency of prayer!

Jesus prayed before He chose His twelve disciples. Esther prayed before she went before the king. Nehemiah prayed before he went to Jerusalem to rebuild the walls. David prayed before he ran into battle. In every situation, prayer helped prepare the way so that the vital work could be effectively done.

We don't know which fields need which attention. But the "Lord of the harvest" does. We don't control the plan. We're not out for the credit. "Neither the one who plants nor the one who waters is anything, but only God who gives the growth" (1 Cor. 3:7).

Pray for Him to raise up and send laborers to tell the people in your world about Jesus. One of them, hopefully, is you. But pray for more. Don't worry how He's going to do it. He has perfect knowledge of all things and has been planning the details since the foundation of the world. Just trust the Lord and pray, and then obey whatever He tells you to do. But prayer is step one. Would you be willing to start praying for this? For your community?

Pray for the harvest. After praying for workers, start praying for each step of their work. Pray for the specific people who need to be reached (1 Tim. 2:1–4). Pray for God to give the workers His compassionate heart for people who don't know Christ (Rom. 5:5). Pray for open doors so the gospel can be shared (Col. 4:2–4). Pray for the boldness and clarity to share its truth (Eph. 6:19–20). Pray for the Holy Spirit to open hearts to the simplicity of belief (Rom. 10:9–13). Pray for new believers to grow up into spiritual maturity and become faithful, fruitful followers of Jesus (Col. 1:9–10).

Pray for workers to train up workers. The task of reaching the world with the gospel is not up to us. That's God's job. "The Lord of the harvest" will bring in His harvest. But we must be obedient, not only to be His workers, but to train up and prepare new workers. New disciples. God's plan is to reach the world, not through addition, but through multiplication. Not through converts alone, but through the explosive growth of faithful disciples who make disciples.

One on one. Two on four. Three on twelve. Small group on small group. When disciples make disciples who make disciples, the multiplied harvest is beyond what we can imagine.

Just do the math. Jesus discipled twelve men over three years. If one person followed His example and went out and made twelve disciples, who then made twelve disciples, and it kept going, we could reach the whole world in thirty years.

But even if one person poured into only two people a year—helping them come to Christ, to read and obey God's Word, and then learn to abide in Him—your one-year investment would theoretically result in two new disciples. If the three of you then continued by discipling two people a year, who then started discipling others, the number of disciples after fifteen years would be more than thirty thousand. After twenty years, a million. After thirty years, a billion.

A billion. What a harvest. An abundant, beautiful harvest. We clearly can't reach the world by addition, but we can do it through His discipleship math.

Not everyone will listen. Not everyone will stick with it or grow to maturity. Not everyone will follow through. Jesus knew Judas would not last. But we can all still focus on one or two. Will you pray to the Lord of the harvest to send out workers? To reach just one or two? And doesn't the Lord want you to be one of those workers He sends?

If it sounds like more than you can do, don't worry about it. Just pray about it.

Then be open to whatever God leads you to do. Can you pray with compassion for those who live nearby you, who work or go to church with you? Those who are living like sheep without a shepherd? Needing someone to introduce them to Christ? To help them grow in Christ?

Pray for your own family, your parents, your siblings, your children, your grandchildren, maybe even a spouse who's hungry to grow spiritually but doesn't know how. Pray!

Then pray for Jesus to send out the workers. Imagine the Lord using you and your humble investment in one or two—in just a few—to change the world over the next generations.

God alone knows who is ready to go to the next level. Ask the Lord to show you where He wants you to focus your prayers and your compassionate service. Pray for His Spirit to show you someone to take out to lunch, or to buy a cup of coffee, or to invite into your home for a starter conversation. Pray for the harvest today. Pray for workers today.

The Lord of the harvest, your Father, deeply cares and will hear your prayers.

Heavenly Father, Lord of the harvest, I pray to You today for workers in Your harvest field. Prepare Your fields. Prepare Your workers. Prepare the soil and send Your Word. Raise up the people You have rescued from death, and send us out to share Your life-giving message with others. Prepare us, Your workers, to do what only You can do through us. Give us eyes to see Your harvest in the eyes of those around us. Lead us, help us, show us, Lord Jesus. Amen.

Going Deeper

1 Thessalonians 1:2–6 • 2 Timothy 2:15 • Hebrews 13:20–21

49

SHARING THE WORLD'S GREATEST NEWS

HOW DO I TELL OTHERS ABOUT JESUS?

He said to them, "Go into all the world and preach the gospel to all creation." Mark 16:15

One of the greatest joys of life is getting to share the best news in the world. The good news of the gospel of Jesus is infinitely more important than anything else we could talk about with anyone. The world's good news is temporary. The gospel is eternal. The world offers short-term relief with a price tag hanging on it. The gospel offers long-term joy and lasting peace at no cost. The world offers conditional love from sinful people. But the gospel offers perfect love through Jesus—the most loving person to walk the earth.

The Bible says to be "ready at any time to give a defense to anyone who asks you for a reason for the hope that is in you" (1 Pet. 3:15). Not to "quarrel," but to be "gentle" and "patient" (2 Tim. 2:24). You can't argue anyone into heaven. It's ineffective and doesn't work. Simply share the truth, trusting the Holy Spirit to work in their hearts.

Jesus modeled this beautifully. In John 4, during His encounter with a Samaritan woman at a well, He demonstrated how to engage someone respectfully in a difficult gospel conversation. This was someone of a different gender, nationality, background, and tradition. Jews and Samaritans were *enemies*, in fact. They didn't interact. And yet Jesus initiated a conversation with her.

Surprised by His audacity, the woman at first became defensive. She repeatedly gave Him reasons why she was not open to Him or His message. But her resistance didn't bother Jesus. He remained very patient. Gently persistent. He knew she needed the gospel much more than she needed the water she was drawing from the well. So He masterfully connected her felt need with her deeper need. He drew her in with sincere compassion and kindness.

Though she remained guarded, He gently exposed her hidden sin and then offered her the hope of the gospel through Him. The Holy Spirit was at work. By the end of their meeting, she had completely changed her mind about Jesus and was excited to share with everyone in her city about Him. Her testimony went on to greatly impact the people around her.

God's Word says to "let your speech always be gracious, seasoned with salt, so that you may know how you should answer each person" (Col. 4:6). Your curiosity and initiative, your gracious speech, and your kind patience with people's skepticism can be captivating to a lost world, offering them help and hope through Jesus. Just listening and sharing, not arguing over secondary issues. You don't need to be a master communicator or an impressive Bible scholar. The Holy Spirit is able to give you the words to say (Luke 12:11–12), convict people of their sin (John 16:8), open their eyes to spiritual truth (1 Cor. 2:11–12), and draw them to salvation (John 6:44; Titus 3:5). "They may come to their senses and escape the trap of the devil, who has taken them captive to do his will" (2 Tim. 2:26).

Here are five effective ways you can share the gospel with others:

Share your testimony. People can argue with your beliefs but not your story. Both the woman at the well and the apostle Paul used their personal testimonies to reach many people with the gospel. You can too!

Share the gospel using one verse. Sometimes the most efficient and effective way to communicate the heart of God to someone is by walking them slowly through a single verse. John 3:16, for example, explains the gospel succinctly. Other verses include Romans 6:23, Romans 10:9, Acts 2:38, Acts 16:31, and 2 Corinthians 5:21.

Share the gospel using a tract. Gospel tracts are small, inexpensive, printed versions of the good news that you can easily hand a stranger or read along with them during a conversation. They can be a helpful tool to guide the conversation or to leave for someone to read later.

Share the gospel through the lens of relationships. The gospel is all about relationships. Talk about it this way. God created us for a *relationship* with Him. Sin separated us from our *relationship* with God. We cannot reconcile this *relationship* on our own by good deeds. God lovingly sent Jesus to rescue us back into a *relationship* by living a perfect life, dying for our sins on the cross, and rising again from the grave. Jesus offers a restored *relationship* to anyone who repents of their sins and places their faith in Him.

Share the gospel using the "Romans Road." The following six verses from the book of Romans have long been used as an effective roadmap for walking someone through the gospel message.

Romans 3:10—"There is no one righteous, not even one." This poses the question, "Why is everyone unrighteous?" The next verse answers that question.

Romans 3:23—"For all have sinned and fall short of the glory of God." Question: "So if we're all unrighteous, what did God do about it?"

Romans 5:8—"But God proves his own love for us in that while we were still sinners, Christ died for us." Question: "Why did Christ have to die?"

Romans 6:23—"For the wages of sin is death, but the gift of God is eternal life in Christ Jesus our Lord." Question: "So how do I get this eternal life?"

Romans 10:9–10—"If you confess with your mouth, 'Jesus is Lord,' and believe in your heart that God raised him from the dead, you will be saved. One believes with the heart, resulting in righteousness, and one confesses with the mouth, resulting in salvation." Question: "Can anyone do this?"

Romans 10:13—"Everyone who calls on the name of the Lord will be saved."

Underline these verses in your Bible or memorize them easily to share with someone, along with your testimony. That's being ready to spread the gospel!

Knowing the Holy Spirit is with you, do not be surprised when He starts using the simple gospel message and your simple story to reach a person's heart for Jesus. If God opens their eyes and they start to express a desire to be saved, be ready to lead them in a simple prayer like this:

"Jesus, I know that I have sinned against You and deserve God's judgment. I believe You died on the cross to pay for my sins and rose again from the dead. I choose now to turn away from my sins and ask for Your forgiveness. Jesus, I'm making You the Lord and Boss of my life. Change me and help me to live the rest of my life for You. Thank You for giving me a home in heaven with You when I die."

Watching God use you to help someone come to know Christ is *THE* most exhilarating and life-changing experience on earth. It never gets old! When you see a heart change as God makes someone into a new person, you'll be amazed all over again at the power of the gospel. So stay open to the leading of the Holy Spirit. Keep praying and abiding in Jesus. God can do great things through your life and your willingness to share Him with others.

Not only will someone else's life never be the same. Neither will yours.

Father, I thank You for how Jesus has personally changed my life. Please use me, my story, and the truth of Scripture to reach others with the gospel. Prepare my heart and open doors. Give me courage and clarity in my speech. Change lives through me. In Jesus' name. Amen.

Going Deeper

John 4:39–42 • 1 Corinthians 2:1–5 • 1 Thessalonians 2:8

50

Making True Disciples

What is the main mission of a disciple?

"As the Father has sent me, I also send you." John 20:21

When someone comes to Christ, this is only the beginning! What a joy to see someone become a new person in Christ, right before our eyes! But it's important to recognize that any new believer is a spiritual infant, needing loving support and gentle attention from spiritual mothers and fathers and older brothers and sisters. Like our own children, they need protection, people who won't do anything to make them stumble (Rom. 14:21; Matt. 18:6). They need mature believers around them who can identify their needs and help them grow in the Word and in their walk with Christ. To grow into mature believers.

This is the end goal of discipleship.

Paul said he passionately proclaimed Christ and taught people about Christ with the goal of presenting them "mature in Christ" (Col. 1:28). But what do mature believers actually look like?

For starters, they don't survive only on the spiritual milk that you and others feed them, but they're becoming able to feed themselves the spiritual meat of the Word (Heb. 5:12–14). They're not only getting a good handle on the truth of what they believe but are teaching others as well (Eph. 4:11–12).

They're growing in their discernment between good and evil (Rom. 12:9). Their mouths are not filled with foolish, toxic speech anymore but are instead becoming fountains of purity, encouragement, and blessing (Eph. 4:29). They're developing restraint and self-control (James 3:2), walking in unity instead of division (Eph. 4:13), and increasing in their capacity to love others (2 Pet. 1:5–8).

They're becoming "complete, lacking nothing" (James 1:4), "equipped for every good work" (2 Tim. 3:17). Basically, they love Jesus, act like Jesus, and serve others like Jesus.

Those who are becoming mature in Christ are ALL-IN for Jesus!

And why shouldn't they be? Why shouldn't *any* of us be? Because Jesus is ALL-IN for us!

Hear it in His Great Commission: "All authority has been given to me in heaven and on earth. Go, therefore, and make disciples of all nations, baptizing them in the name of the Father and of the Son and of the Holy Spirit, teaching them to observe everything I have commanded you. And remember, I am with you always, to the end of the age" (Matt. 28:18–20).

From all eternity, God the Father has been ALL-IN regarding His intentions. The Great Commission is the natural continuation of His wholehearted purposes. It's His way of calling and equipping imperfect people to be wholeheartedly devoted to Him, to experience for themselves and then extend to others what knowing and following Jesus is all about. Consider the ALL-IN nature of His words:

"All authority has been given to me"—ALL rights and ALL power are His.
"In heaven and on earth"—in ALL places.
"Go, therefore, and make disciples"—go make ALL-IN followers of Christ.
"Of all nations"—of ALL the world.
"Baptizing them"—ALL of them.
"In the name of the Father and of the Son and of the Holy Spirit"—ALL of God.
"Teaching them to observe everything I have commanded you"—ALL of His Word.
"And remember, I am with you always"—ALL the time.
"To the end of the age"—ALL the way home.

Why would we not want to be ALL-IN on this all-consuming endeavor, seeing that Almighty God, all day long, is ALL-IN on it too? Growing up wholehearted disciples.

The Great Commission is the most epic command and calling of all time. We as His followers are not here merely to attend church and do religious things, to soak up the blessings of salvation while we wait for His return. He's challenged us to get busy and stay busy about discipleship. Not just to know Him but to make Him known. Not just to *be* His disciple but to *make* His disciples. To fully follow Him by helping others fully follow Him as well. He is calling all His disciples to be greatly focused and greatly committed to the greatest agenda for the greatest cause.

His Great Commission!

It's what disciples do. Not just those who've been to seminary. Not just the ones who preach in pulpits. The Great Commission is for every born-again, baptized believer who is devoted to following Christ and obeying His commands.

Being committed to the Great Commission doesn't mean you need to quit your job, sell the farm, wear sandals in the Holy Land, or serve on staff at a church. Nothing outwardly may change at all, other than God being first in your heart now. But as you daily walk in an abiding, obedient relationship with Him, as He daily bears fruit through you, He will start using your time and talents, your responsibilities, relationships, and resources for His higher purposes. To advance His kingdom for His glory. To help other people come to know Him and be His disciple too. He will lead, and you will follow.

You might become a Jesus-loving, gospel-sharing, people-serving, disciple-making used car salesman, football coach, firefighter, or police officer. You might become a gray-headed, independent movie producer who starts making disciples on sets while making movies that share Jesus. You might become a sold-out plumber who helps people find living water, or a Spirit-filled manure salesman who shares how God can bring fruitful life out of the stench of death. We serve a perfect God who uses imperfect people full of Jesus to share how He has changed them. We are all a work in progress. But He can plow straight rows with ugly oxen. He actively uses the nail-scarred hands and the bloody feet of the body of Christ every day as we love Him and serve Him.

Will you be someone who's willing to give God your "Yes" today? Someone who's simply walking with Jesus? Someone who's willing to obey, even with trembling hands? Someone the Lord knows He can call on? Someone who will do what

He says and go where He sends? Even if you're unsure, even if you're afraid to get involved, will you take stock of the ALL-IN promises that God has made to be with you? To help you? To exercise His own eternal authority on your behalf? To provide His Holy Spirit to guide you every step of the way? To fill you and empower you and guide you from within?

As God's beloved child, you are never alone and you will never be left alone. You stand on the awesome shoulders of God's never-weakening plans and promises. You are undergirded by the resurrection power of the same God who spoke the galaxies into being and raised Jesus Christ from the dead. You are locking arms with the great "cloud of witnesses" (Heb. 12:1) who've faithfully marched to the beat of His Great Commission for centuries past, all over the world.

You are called to this. You'll be given what you need for this. You can do this.

The Lord God Himself is behind you. With all His heart.

Dear Father in heaven, there is nothing You can't do. You have proven Yourself and Your mighty power, not only throughout history but throughout my life. Produce in me a new resolve for being part of Your calling for making disciples. Show me how. Show me who. And I will follow You. I will dare to believe You. I can't wait to give You glory for what You alone can do through me, as You pour the same truth and grace You've given me into someone else. I pray in the name of Jesus. Amen.

Going Deeper

Luke 24:46–49 • Acts 1:7–8 • 1 Timothy 6:12–16

51

STEPS OF DISCIPLESHIP

HOW DO I START MAKING DISCIPLES?

"Go, therefore, and make disciples of all nations." Matthew 28:19

Do you doubt that God could greatly use you to make disciples? Don't be afraid. He prefers the underdog over the top dog. He often recruits the poor over the rich. The undignified over the amplified. The least and the last. The most underwhelming and unlikely of all (1 Cor. 1:26–31).

Why? Because they are more humble and more teachable. More grateful and willing to serve. More likely to give God the credit instead of basking in their own glory.

God chose fearful Gideon, washed-up Moses, little-brother David, and humble Mary. He picked the least likely woman in Samaria to evangelize her village (John 4:39–42), and He chose a once-naked, homeless, demon-possessed guy to take the gospel back to his hometown (Luke 8:38–39). Go figure.

The very last option to us may be God's very first choice. But He will *always* choose available disciples who are willing to obey His Great Commission. To make disciples.

The first part of making disciples is being a humble disciple yourself. You can't challenge people to be ALL-IN for Jesus if you're half-hearted and only half-interested in Him yourself. True disciple-making is more than having words to say but providing an example to follow. You don't need to be perfect. Nobody's perfect! But are you living with hidden sin? Are you resisting His Word? Are you not really convinced the gospel can change people's lives?

Before jumping into a teaching role, you may first need to ask someone to help disciple *you*. That's okay. There's so much to be gained by humbling yourself to learn under someone whose example can consistently keep pointing you to Jesus.

But when you're ready, the Lord will prompt you to become the one who mentors someone else, sharing rich conversations with them and teaching them to read and obey God's Word.

It might be someone in your church. Your child or that younger friend of theirs who's always over at your house anyway. It might be a neighbor from across the street or in the next building. It might be someone at work. A customer. A new acquaintance. Anybody God chooses. Stay sensitive to the Lord to point out someone who's hungry for truth, who's asking deeper questions than most people, who's seeking guidance for their life. The Lord will lead you!

What an incredible honor it would be to walk with someone through their entire discipleship journey, all the way from the start, from the moment when God first cracked open the hardened soil of their hearts. Jesus did this. He stuck with His disciples until He knew they were ready to go make disciples themselves. Paul did it with Timothy.

But often, these discipleship relationships are just for a season. You're there for only a part of their journey. Maybe a year. Maybe a decade. Planting. Watering. Trusting God to give them (and you!) a time of real growth as you walk together (1 Cor. 3:7).

Some people, as God leads you toward them, will get to hear the gospel message from your lips for the first time. For others, it may be the fifteenth time, but when you share it, the Holy Spirit removes the blinders and they believe (Acts 16:14). You may help some get baptized, get their first Bible, or learn how to study it and apply it. Others will be fellow believers at church you encourage weekly. You may be the one God uses to comfort them or help restore them out of a dark valley. You may see some grow to full maturity. Others you may send out to plant churches and change nations! This is kingdom living. Abundant disciple making. Worthy of all our lives! Whoever God sends to you, be faithful in that season and be open to staying involved in their lives.

Just be praying specifically right now for God to place one or more people in your path that you can help take their next step. Ask God to make it clear as you pray.

When you meet with people, there are many ways to assist in their growth. Everyone always has a need of the moment. Ask sincere questions to try discerning their current situation—where they are, how they're doing. What can you pray about with them? Both spiritually and practically. Sometimes people are willing to open up only after *you* have opened up and demonstrated sincerity, or after you've met a genuine need in their lives. Be patient.

It's always right to help people get into the Word. Read through Scripture together, work through a book (like this one), or discuss your quiet times with the Lord. Spend time in honest conversation. Pray for one another. Share each other's joys and burdens, applying the Word to them. Regardless, seek to model humility, kindness, patience, and loving generosity. And repentance. Ask the Lord for specific requests. Don't try to impress. Be sincere but bold in prayer.

You may find, as you get to know someone, that they've never truly believed the gospel for salvation. If not, you can start praying for them, sharing your story, and hopefully enjoying the thrill of watching them receive Christ.

Or maybe they've embraced the gospel but are not currently worshiping in a good local church. Invite them to your church to sit with you. Or maybe they've never been baptized. Isn't that a stated part of the Great Commission? "Go . . . make disciples . . . baptizing them" (Matt. 28:19). You can be the one to encourage them to talk with their church leadership about baptism. Don't assume they have a copy of the Bible that's a translation they can understand. If they don't, could there be any better gift for you to give someone to learn more about God?

But don't limit disciple-making to a six-week Bible study in a church. The process of "teaching them to observe everything I have commanded you" (Matt. 28:20) can happen in the most ordinary encounters and conversations. At the coffee shop. At school. After ball practice. In the break room. In your living room. Over months and even years.

Let this person into your life and world. Give them an example worth following. Show them how you manage your time or choose better activities and entertainment that honors the Lord and your testimony. Talk with them about how you handle money and make decisions from a biblical perspective. Ask them if they have any questions. Answer what you can and prayerfully search God's Word and good counsel for what you don't know.

Walk in humility. Nothing gets left out of lordship. He is King of everything. Of all of us.

No, this is not easy. It's supposed to cost you something and take time. It's an eternal investment and will eat into some parts of your schedule that you once reserved for lesser, more self-serving things. But it will be exciting, new, and absolutely worth it. Here and in eternity.

No joy can compare to seeing someone fall in love with Jesus and being powerfully shaped into His image. The apostle John spoke about those he had won to Christ and said, "I have no greater joy than this: to hear that my children are walking in truth" (3 John 4). From a man who walked with Jesus and saw so many miracles, that's a lot of joy!

It's the disciple-maker's passion and prize.

Whatever you hope it could become, it will be even better than that.

Heavenly Father, make me a disciple who walks in integrity and makes disciples of others. Give me the courage I need and make me humble and vulnerable enough to believe You can use me. I offer myself to You for the greatest spiritual adventure of all—for Your glory. Help me be part of fulfilling Your Great Commission, in Jesus' name. Amen.

Going Deeper

Deuteronomy 6:4–7 • Psalm 145:4–7 • 3 John 2–4

52

Following Jesus to the End

What does it take to finish well as His disciple?

"This good news of the kingdom will be proclaimed in all the world as a testimony to all nations, and then the end will come." Matthew 24:14

Pray first that God will speak to your heart!

At the end of His earthly ministry, after training them for three years, Jesus gave His Great Commission to eleven faithful disciples who had laid aside every hindrance and were ready to lead others faithfully (Matt. 28:16). It's encouraging He hadn't sent them out at the *beginning* of His ministry to "make disciples of all nations" (v. 19) before they were ready, before they understood who He was, what God could do through them, or what discipleship fully meant.

A disciple is a devoted *follower*. A loyal *apprentice*. One who intentionally follows closely behind and imitates their teacher, their rabbi. When their rabbi takes a step, his disciple takes a step into the footprint left behind. It's a step-in-step relationship. A disciple's feet should be covered with the dust of their rabbi's sandals.

Jesus perfectly modeled the teacher and rabbi role for His disciples. He didn't just invite them to follow His words. His invitation was, "Come, follow Me." *Walk with Me. Follow what I say and what I do. Learn and grow as you step in My steps.*

Think about how this simple understanding of discipleship sheds light on the entire ministry of Jesus. Now His invitations make even more sense. What were the steps Jesus had taken that He was later asking His disciples to take?

First, as the Son of God in heaven, Jesus willingly laid down His eternal rights (Phil. 2:5–8), His divine glory (John 17:5), His beloved relationship with His Father (v. 23), and all His heavenly possessions (2 Cor. 8:9), so that He could obey His Father, come to earth, and lay down His life for us. He gave up everything to do the will of His Father. All out of faithful love for Him and us.

What did Jesus then invite His disciples to do? *The same.* He called them to lay aside any encumbrance that would keep them from fully following Him, including their possessions (Luke 14:33), their relationships, and even their own lives (v. 26)—exactly as He had done before coming to earth.

When He said, "The Son of Man did not come to be served, but to serve" (Matt. 20:28), He was simultaneously challenging them to die to their own greatness and embrace the role of a servant. As He stepped toward the cross, He said, "If anyone wants to follow after me, let him deny himself, take up his cross daily, and follow me" (Luke 9:23), He was only telling them to do what He had already modeled for them.

Near the end of His time with them, when He knew He had loved them to the end and was soon to return to His Father, Jesus humbly washed His disciples' feet, saying, "If I, your Lord and Teacher, have washed your feet, you also ought to wash one another's feet. For I have given you an example, that you also should do just as I have done for you" (John 13:14–15).

Then He shifted gears. Having cleaned His rabbi dust off their feet, He revealed something new to them. They could not take the next step with Him. "Where I am going, you cannot follow me now, but you will follow later" (John 13:36). The one place they (and we) couldn't follow Him was in doing what He alone could do—to lay down His life as our substitute—to represent us in His role as high priest. When He was crucified, we were therefore crucified, because of His representation. When He died, we died. When He was buried, we were buried. When He was raised, we were raised with Him (Rom. 6:3–11).

Yet He was still discipling these disciples. In His horrific suffering, Jesus showed how to glorify God even during seasons of great pain and persecution. As Peter wrote to believers, "You were called to this, because Christ also suffered for you, leaving you an example, that you should follow in his steps" (1 Pet. 2:21).

After His resurrection, Jesus said, "As the Father has sent me, I also send you" (John 20:21). They followed His example and went, imitating His ministry—lovingly preaching the gospel from city to city by the power of the Holy Spirit, praying in faith, baptizing believers, serving genuine needs, performing miracles, and teaching the Word of God.

This is the disciple's way—step in step—a much more effective, efficient, and enjoyable way to train people than merely talking at them from a distance. People learn exponentially faster when the truth they hear is wrapped inside a loving relationship and an example they can see and imitate.

Jesus is forever our rabbi and teacher, the first and primary example for anyone to follow, but our lives become His teaching tool when we follow Him in front of others. As Paul said, "Follow my example, even as I also follow the example of Christ" (1 Cor. 11:1 NIV). Where Jesus guides, we go. Where He steps, we step. What He loves, we love. What He hates, we hate. What He says, we say. How He served, we serve. Where His Word and His Spirit lead, we follow. Then others follow us, just as we follow Christ.

But we must be fully following Jesus ourselves if we ask others to follow us.

If you're new to faith, if you're not ready to spiritually lead, then patiently stay focused on becoming His disciple during this season—humbling yourself, staying teachable, walking in obedience, and forsaking any sin or encumbrance that is in the way of your walk. Keep sharing your story and the gospel, of course, but keep abiding in Him daily, learning to obey His Word, and continuing to grow.

The time will come. You'll know it. Others will see and confirm it. The more surrendered and faithful you are, the more He will pour through you into others. Every step closer to Christ you take, the more steps you can help others take.

Where are you in your journey? Do you need to be discipled, or are you ready to disciple others? Is there anything in your life holding you back from being wholehearted in your walk with Jesus?

God's Word says, "Let us also lay aside every encumbrance and the sin which so easily entangles us, and let us run with endurance the race that is set before us, fixing our eyes on Jesus, the author and perfecter of faith, who for the joy set before Him endured the cross, despising the shame, and has sat down at the right hand of the throne of God" (Heb. 12:1–2 NASB).

As His disciples, we will one day be rewarded for every ounce of pain, suffering, or persecution we have endured for His sake. Every temporary right, worldly possession, or hindering relationship we laid down for Christ will be worth it in eternity. We must keep seeking Him in prayer and in His Word, always ready to serve Him as He walks ahead of us and shepherds us forward.

Our God has given us everything we need to be found faithful to Him (2 Pet. 1:3). We have a perfect example in our Savior who has reconciled us completely back to God. We have a loving Father who has blessed us with every spiritual blessing, including constant access to Him in prayer. We have the Holy Spirit as our constant companion, comfort, and help. We have new identities in Christ as God's beloved children. We have the fellowship and support of other believers. We have the same rich, eternal inheritance as Jesus. He is *for* us. He is *with* us. He is *in* us. He will never leave us or forsake us.

This world is passing away. Eternity is the priority. We must adjust accordingly. It won't be that long before we'll be home with Him forever. So let's embrace the life of His devoted disciple. Let us throw off any hindrance, run with resolute endurance, and intentionally reach this next generation for Christ. The Great Commission will be fulfilled through discipleship, not merely evangelism. We must help the body of Christ train and send mature disciples to the nations, who will be found faithful even in the fire of persecution.

Our prayer and expected hope is to stand before the throne of God, clothed in Christ's righteousness and grateful that we gave our lives wholeheartedly to Him and to His worthy name. We will join those who stepped into eternity before us, as well as those who stepped into eternity following us, together enjoying our Savior, beholding His glory forever . . . not just step in step, but face to Face.

Will you join us? Let it be so, Lord Jesus.

"Now to him who is able to protect you from stumbling and to make you stand in the presence of his glory, without blemish and with great joy, to the only God our Savior, through Jesus Christ our Lord, be glory, majesty, power, and authority before all time, now and forever. Amen" (Jude 24–25). To God be the glory!

THE GREAT COMMISSION

Jesus came near and said to them,
"All authority has been given to me in heaven and on earth.
Go, therefore, and make disciples of all nations,
baptizing them in the name
of the Father and of the Son and of the Holy Spirit,
teaching them to observe all that I have commanded you.
And remember, I am with you always, to the end of the age."
Matthew 28:18–20

THE WORD OF GOD IN MY LIFE

Let this proclamation help you to rightly approach the Word of God.

The Bible is the Word of God.

It is holy, inerrant, infallible, and completely authoritative. *(Proverbs 30:5–6; John 17:17; Psalm 119:89)*

It is profitable for teaching, reproving, correcting, and training me in righteousness. *(2 Timothy 3:16)*

It matures and equips me to be ready for every good work. *(2 Timothy 3:17)*

It is a lamp to my feet and a light to my path. *(Psalm 119:105)*

It makes me wiser than my enemies. *(Psalm 119:97–100)*

It brings me stability during the storms of my life. *(Matthew 7:24–27)*

If I believe its truth, I will be set free. *(John 8:32)*

If I hide it in my heart, I will be protected in times of temptation. *(Psalm 199:11)*

If I continue in it, I will become a true disciple. *(John 8:31)*

If I meditate on it, I will become successful. *(Joshua 1:8)*

If I keep it, I will be rewarded and my love perfected. *(Psalm 19:7–11; 1 John 2:5)*

It is the living, powerful, discerning Word of God. *(Hebrews 4:12)*

It is the Sword of the Spirit. *(Ephesians 6:17)*

It is sweeter than honey and more desirable than gold. *(Psalm 19:10)*

It is indestructible and forever settled in Heaven. *(2 Corinthians 13:7–8; Psalm 119:89)*

It is absolutely true with no mixture of error. *(John 17:17; Titus 1:2)*

It is absolutely true about God. *(Romans 3:4; Romans 16:25, 27; Colossians 1)*

It is absolutely true about man. *(Jeremiah 17:9; Psalm 8:4–6)*

It is absolutely true about sin. *(Romans 3:23)*

It is absolutely true about salvation. *(Acts 4:12; Romans 10:9)*

It is absolutely true about Heaven and Hell. *(Revelation 21:8; Psalm 119:89)*

Lord, open my eyes that I may see truth and my ears to hear truth.
Open my heart to receive it by faith.
Renew my mind to keep it in hope.
Surrender my will that I may live it with love.
Remind me that I am responsible when I hear it.

Help me desire to obey what You say through it.
Transform my life that I may know it.
Burden my heart that I may share it.

Speak now, Lord.
Give me a passion to know and follow Your will.
Nothing more. Nothing less. Nothing else.

CHOOSING A CHURCH

God wants His children devoting themselves to a solid fellowship of believers. Choosing the right church home is vitally important. It can greatly influence your life and family long-term. A solid body of believers is a taste of heaven. A toxic church should not be your home. No two churches are exactly alike. They have a wide range of styles of leadership, teaching, music, worship, and service. Here are a few tips as you look for a good church home.

1. PRAY FOR GOD TO LEAD YOU. Ask Him to give you wisdom, discernment, and direction. You may live in a region with no options. It may be illegal to follow Christ in your country. But God can provide anything, anywhere, and supply even a small group of genuine believers to privately grow with you. Read Acts 2:42 and pray for help!

2. DO YOUR HOMEWORK. If possible, research their websites, look at their beliefs, and look for signs of health, growth, and spiritual vitality. Consider visiting several churches in your area until you find one that truly aligns with what you need and value.

3. LOOK FOR A BIBLICALLY SOLID CHURCH. Join a church that believes Jesus is God's Son and the only way of salvation, and that the Bible is the true, infallible Word of God. If they don't study the Bible or if they claim other religious books are just as true, then leave.

4. LOOK FOR A UNIFIED, LOVING CHURCH. True believers are known by their love. Every church will have its share of problems as they minister to broken people, but if a church's leaders fight on a regular basis about secondary things, it would likely be better to raise your family in a different, unified church somewhere else.

5. LOOK FOR A FRUITFUL CHURCH. Look for a church where the gospel is being shared and people are coming to Christ. If you never see any life-change, baptisms, or growing disciples of Christ being formed, then keep looking.

6. LOOK FOR A PLACE YOU CAN GROW AND SERVE. A good church will help you grow spiritually. Hearing the Word regularly, worshiping, and fellowshiping with other believers should be a very edifying experience. You should also be able to find ways to serve that will bless you and the people you are serving.

7. LOOK FOR A PRAYING CHURCH. Jesus said, "My house will be called a house of prayer" (Matt. 21:13). True believers will pray together on a regular basis and see answers to those prayers. If prayer is an afterthought in a church and no answers abound, that's not a good sign.

8. FOLLOW THE HOLY SPIRIT. If multiple churches teach the Bible and check all the boxes as good options, but God gives you a peace about one and a red flag about others, then trust Him by faith and follow His peace (Col. 3:15). When you find a solid church home, it will be worth the search and the wait. Don't give up!

PRAYER BOARD

"Ask, and it will be given to you; seek, and you will find; knock, and it will be opened to you." Matthew 7:7 NASB

God rewards those who seek Him. He knows your heart, your burdens, and your true needs, and He invites you to seek Him regarding them as part of your growing faith and daily relationship with Him. He is Lord, and His responses and timing are always perfect. Use this page to start writing down pressing needs. Then pray daily for His help "in the name of Jesus," and make a record of when He answers those prayers. Let His responses build your faith as you keep waiting on other answers and seeking Him for greater things.

Practical Needs for God's Provision and Intervention

____

____

____

____

Decisions Needing God's Wisdom, Clarity, and Direction

____

____

____

____

Problems and Worries Needing God's Peace or Intervention

Relationship Issues Needing God's Guidance and Grace

Spiritual Needs for Revelation, Direction, and Breakthrough

ABOUT THE AUTHORS

STEPHEN KENDRICK is a writer, speaker, and film producer with a passion for sharing the truth and love of Jesus among the nations. He produces the Kendrick Brothers' films and has cowritten (with Alex) the *New York Times* bestsellers *The Love Dare, The Resolution for Men,* and *The Battle Plan for Prayer*. Stephen is a frequent speaker on marriage, fatherhood, discipleship, and prayer. He and his wife, Jill, have six children.

ALEX KENDRICK is an accomplished author, actor, and film director, whose credits include *Facing the Giants, Fireproof, Courageous, War Room, Overcomer,* and most recently, *The Forge*. A creative artist with a pastor's heart, Alex speaks internationally on the power of film and the surpassing power of Christ. He and his wife, Christina, have six children.